Mmmm...
Soup

Mmmm...
Soup

First published in 2011

LOVE FOOD is an imprint of Parragon Books Ltd

Parragon
Queen Street House
4 Queen Street
Bath BA1 1HE, UK

ISBN: 978-1-4454-2442-2

Printed in China

Internal design by Talking Design
Introduction by Linda Doeser

Notes for the Reader
This book uses both metric and imperial measurements. Follow the same units of
measurement throughout; do not mix metric and imperial. All spoon measurements are
level: teaspoons are assumed to be 5 ml, and tablespoons are assumed to be 15 ml.
Unless otherwise stated, milk is assumed to be full fat, eggs and individual vegetables are
medium, and pepper is freshly ground black pepper.

The times given are an approximate guide only. Preparation times differ according to the
techniques used by different people and the cooking times may also vary from those
given. Optional ingredients, variations or serving suggestions have not been included in
the calculations.

Recipes using raw or very lightly cooked eggs should be avoided by infants, the elderly,
pregnant women, convalescents and anyone suffering from an illness. Pregnant and
breastfeeding women are advised to avoid eating peanuts and peanut products.
Sufferers from nut allergies should be aware that some of the ready-made ingredients
used in the recipes in this book may contain nuts. Always check the packaging before use.

contents

introduction

Home-made soup is the ultimate comfort food, yet it is one of the easiest dishes to make. Its versatility is almost endless as it may be based on vegetables, meat, poultry, fish or seafood. Some soups are delicately flavoured and elegant, while others are robust and substantial. Chilled soups are a delightful summer treat and nothing is more welcome on a cold winter's evening than a steaming bowl of home-made broth.

The basis of a really flavoursome soup is a good stock. Time is at a premium in this modern world and, fortunately, there are some good-quality ready-made stocks available. Cubes are very convenient and keep for quite a long time, but they are often very salty. Price is a guide, although not invariably, to their quality. Liquid stocks and concentrates often have a better flavour and the best ones have no additives or salt.

Making your own stock isn't difficult but is time-consuming. Life is too short for non-professional cooks to saw and roast beef bones, bring them slowly to the boil with vegetables – about 1 hour – and then simmer for anything up to 3 hours, before skimming and straining and clarifying the next day. However, there are some short-cuts that will produce a very acceptable stock to enhance the flavour of home-made soups without your spending hours in the kitchen.

Many supermarkets sell stock or stew packs containing chicken wings, onion, carrot and sometimes other vegetables, such as leeks. Put one or two of these into a large saucepan, depending on how much stock you require, add any extra vegetables if you like and a bouquet garni and pour in water to cover by about 5 cm/2 inches. Bring to the boil over a low heat, skimming off any scum that rises to the surface, then simmer gently, uncovered and without stirring, for 1–2 hours. Strain through a muslin-lined sieve into a bowl, then ideally chill in the refrigerator overnight and spoon off the fat that will have set on the surface the next day. If you want to use the stock immediately, blot up the globules of fat from the surface with kitchen paper. You can also make a chicken stock in the same way using the carcass and trimmings from a roast chicken and a selection of vegetables, such as onion, leek, carrots, celery sticks and even lettuce leaves.

You can make a quick beef stock with 500 g/1 lb 2 oz minced beef, a diced carrot, leek, onion and celery stick and some fresh herb sprigs, such as parsley. Put them into a saucepan, pour in 1.3 litres/2¼ pints water and bring to the boil over a low heat, skimming off any scum that rises to the surface. Partially cover the pan and simmer gently, without stirring, for 1 hour, then strain as above and remove the fat.

Easy vegetable stock can be made by gently cooking a chopped onion, carrot and celery stick, plus any other vegetables you have to hand in 55 g/2 oz butter for 10 minutes. Add some fresh herb sprigs, such as thyme and parsley, pour in 1 litre/1¾ pints water and bring to the boil. Partially cover the pan and simmer gently for 20 minutes. Strain into a bowl.

Vegetable trimmings, such as asparagus stalks and the outer leaves of cauliflower, and cooking water, such as that used for green beans or corncobs, can be added to the stockpot. However, it is best to avoid strong-tasting brassicas, such as cabbage and Brussels sprouts.

Do not season the stock until you are using it to make soup, as salt may become concentrated during cooking, thus spoiling the flavour, and pepper tends to make it cloudy.

Embellishments & accompaniments

- Turn your soup into something special with a dash of wine or fortified wine, such as sherry, Madeira or Marsala. Add it just before serving for extra flavour and aroma. If you want to cook out the alcohol but retain the flavour, allow the soup to bubble for a couple of minutes before serving.

- A sprinkling of chopped fresh herbs or finely grated Parmesan makes an easy garnish and a spoonful of pesto is a great addition to minestrone.

- A swirl of double cream, natural yogurt or crème fraîche looks very attractive in a colourful creamy vegetable soup.

- A sprinkling of caviar or – much less expensive – keta or salmon roe makes a sophisticated garnish for a special fish or shellfish soup.

- For an unusual vegetable garnish, slice 2 carrots into very fine julienne strips and put them into a saucepan. Add water to cover and 2 tablespoons butter. Bring to the boil, then reduce the heat and simmer for about 5 minutes, until tender but still firm to the bite. Drain well.

- Croûtons are a great addition to soups. Cut 55 g/2 oz crustless white bread into 5-mm/¼-inch cubes or, for a special occasion, diamonds, triangles or batons. Melt 55 g/2 oz butter or 2 tablespoons olive or sunflower oil in a frying pan, add the bread and cook, tossing and stirring constantly, for a few minutes, until golden brown all over. Remove with a slotted spoon and drain on kitchen paper. For garlic croûtons, cook a peeled whole garlic clove in the pan for 1–2 minutes, until lightly browned, then remove before adding the bread.

- Fresh bread and rolls are a traditional accompaniment to soup. Most supermarkets sell a huge range, including ciabatta and focaccia – perfect for Italian soups – brioche and baguettes – great for all kinds of soups, particularly French ones – corn bread – ideal for chowders – and, of course, wholemeal, crusty white bread, soda bread and seeded rolls.

crusty white bread

makes 1 medium loaf
- 1 egg
- 1 egg yolk
- lukewarm water, as required
- 500 g/1 lb 2 oz strong white bread flour, plus extra for dusting
- 1½ tsp salt
- 2 tsp sugar
- 1 tsp easy-blend dried yeast
- 25 g/1 oz butter, diced
  sunflower oil, for greasing

1 Place the egg and egg yolk in a jug and beat lightly to mix. Add enough lukewarm water to make up to 300 ml/10 fl oz. Stir well.

2 Place the flour, salt, sugar and yeast in a large bowl. Add the butter and rub it in with your fingertips until the mixture resembles breadcrumbs. Make a well in the centre, add the egg mixture and work to a smooth dough.

3 Turn out on to a lightly floured surface and knead well for about 10 minutes, until smooth. Brush a bowl with oil. Shape the dough into a ball, place it in the bowl and put the bowl into a plastic bag or cover with a damp tea towel. Leave to rise in a warm place for 1 hour, until the dough has doubled in volume.

4 Oil a loaf tin. Turn the dough out on to a lightly floured surface and knead for 1 minute until smooth. Shape the dough the length of the tin and three times the width. Fold the dough into three lengthways and place it in the tin with the join underneath. Cover and leave in a warm place for 30 minutes until it has risen above the tin.

5 Preheat the oven to 220°C/425°F/Gas Mark 7. Bake in the oven for 30 minutes, or until firm and golden brown. Test that the loaf is cooked by tapping on the base with your knuckles – it should sound hollow. Transfer to a wire rack to cool.

wholemeal bread

makes 1 small loaf

- 225 g/8 oz strong wholemeal bread flour, plus extra for dusting
- 1 tbsp skimmed milk powder
- 1 tsp salt
- 2 tbsp soft brown sugar
- 1 tsp easy-blend dried yeast
- 1½ tbsp sunflower oil, plus extra for greasing
- 175 ml/6 fl oz lukewarm water

1 Place the flour, milk powder, salt, sugar and yeast in a large bowl. Pour in the oil and add the water, then mix well to make a smooth dough.

2 Turn out on to a lightly floured surface and knead well for about 10 minutes, until smooth. Brush a bowl with oil. Shape the dough into a ball, place it in the bowl and put the bowl into a plastic bag or cover with a damp tea towel. Leave to rise in a warm place for 1 hour, until the dough has doubled in volume.

3 Oil a 900-g/2-lb loaf tin. Turn the dough out on to a lightly floured surface and knead for 1 minute until smooth. Shape the dough the length of the tin and three times the width. Fold the dough into three lengthways and place it in the tin with the join underneath. Cover and leave in a warm place for 30 minutes until it has risen above the tin.

4 Preheat the oven to 220°C/425°F/Gas Mark 7. Bake in the oven for 30 minutes, or until firm and golden brown. Test that the loaf is cooked by tapping on the base with your knuckles – it should sound hollow. Transfer to a wire rack to cool.

Mmmm...
vegetables

fresh tomato soup with pasta

serves 4

- 1 tbsp olive oil
- 4 large plum tomatoes
- 1 onion, cut into quarters
- 1 garlic clove, thinly sliced
- 1 celery stick, roughly chopped
- 500 ml/18 fl oz chicken stock
- 55 g/2 oz dried soup pasta
- salt and pepper
- chopped fresh flat-leaf parsley, to garnish

1 Pour the oil into a large heavy-based saucepan and add the tomatoes, onion, garlic and celery. Cover and cook over a low heat, occasionally shaking gently, for 45 minutes, until pulpy.

2 Transfer the mixture to a food processor or blender and process to a smooth purée.

3 Push the purée through a sieve into a clean saucepan.

4 Add the stock and bring to the boil. Add the pasta, bring back to the boil and cook for 8–10 minutes, until the pasta is tender but still firm to the bite. Season to taste with salt and pepper.

5 Ladle into warmed bowls, sprinkle with parsley and serve immediately.

italian tomato soup

serves 6

- 300 g/10½ oz sourdough bread
- 100 ml/3½ fl oz chicken stock
- 4 tbsp extra virgin olive oil
- 3 tbsp fresh sage leaves, shredded
- 4 garlic cloves, peeled and finely chopped
- 800 g/1 lb 12 oz canned peeled plum tomatoes
- 1 tsp sugar
- 250 ml/9 fl oz hot water
- salt and pepper
- 55 g/2 oz Parmesan cheese, grated, to serve

1 Chop the bread into rough chunks, about 2.5 cm/1 inch square. Place a heavy-based saucepan over a medium heat. Add the stock, oil and sage and simmer until reduced by half. Add the bread and garlic, increase the heat to high and fry until all the liquid has been soaked up and the bread begins to crisp.

2 Add the tomatoes and sugar, stir and simmer for 15 minutes. Add up to 250 ml/9 fl oz hot water to thin the soup to your preferred consistency (it should be quite thick). Simmer for a further minute. Taste and adjust the seasoning.

3 Ladle into bowls, sprinkle a little Parmesan cheese on top and serve immediately.

tomato & white bean soup

serves 6

- 3 tbsp olive oil
- 450 g/1 lb red onions, chopped
- 1 celery stick with leaves, chopped
- 1 red pepper, deseeded and chopped
- 2 garlic cloves, finely chopped
- 1 kg/2 lb 4 oz plum tomatoes, peeled and chopped
- 1.3 litres/2¼ pints vegetable stock
- 2 tbsp tomato purée
- 1 tsp sugar
- 1 tbsp sweet paprika
- 1 tbsp butter
- 1 tbsp plain flour
- 400 g/14 oz canned cannellini beans, drained and rinsed
- salt and pepper
- 3 tbsp chopped fresh flat-leaf parsley, to garnish

1 Heat the olive oil in a large saucepan. Add the onions, celery, red pepper and garlic and cook over a low heat, stirring occasionally, for 5 minutes, until softened.

2 Increase the heat to medium, add the tomatoes and cook, stirring occasionally, for a further 5 minutes, then pour in the stock. Stir in the tomato purée, sugar and sweet paprika and season to taste with salt and pepper. Bring to the boil, reduce the heat and simmer for 15 minutes.

3 Meanwhile, mash together the butter and flour to a paste in a small bowl with a fork. Stir the paste piece by piece into the soup. Make sure each piece is fully incorporated before adding the next.

4 Add the beans, stir well and simmer for a further 5 minutes, until heated through. Sprinkle with the parsley and serve immediately.

minestrone

serves 4

- 2 tbsp olive oil
- 2 garlic cloves, chopped
- 2 red onions, chopped
- 1 red pepper, deseeded and chopped
- 1 orange pepper, deseeded and chopped
- 400 g/14 oz canned chopped tomatoes
- 1 litre/1¾ pints vegetable stock
- 1 celery stick, chopped
- 400 g/14 oz canned borlotti beans
- 100 g/3½ oz green leafy cabbage, shredded
- 75 g/2¾ oz frozen peas, defrosted
- 1 tbsp chopped fresh parsley
- 75 g/2¾ oz dried vermicelli
- salt and pepper
- freshly grated Parmesan cheese, to garnish

1 Heat the oil in a large saucepan over a medium heat, add the garlic and onions and cook, stirring, for 3 minutes, until slightly softened. Add the red and orange peppers and the chopped tomatoes and cook for a further 2 minutes, stirring. Stir in the stock, then add the celery. Drain and add the borlotti beans along with the cabbage, peas and parsley. Season with salt and pepper. Bring to the boil, then lower the heat and simmer for 30 minutes.

2 Add the vermicelli to the pan. Cook for a further 10–12 minutes, or according to the instructions on the packet. Remove from the heat and ladle into serving bowls. Garnish with freshly grated Parmesan and serve immediately.

black bean soup

serves 6

- 3 tbsp corn oil
- 1 large onion, chopped
- 2 celery sticks, chopped
- 2 garlic cloves, chopped
- 450 g/1 lb dried black beans or black-eyed beans, soaked overnight in cold water to cover, and drained
- 2.5 litres/4½ pints vegetable stock
- ¾ tsp cayenne pepper
- 5 tbsp lemon juice
- 2 tbsp red wine vinegar
- 2 tbsp dry sherry
- 4 hard-boiled eggs, roughly chopped
- salt and pepper
- chopped celery leaves, to garnish
- grated Cheddar cheese, to serve

1 Heat the oil in a large saucepan. Add the onion, celery and garlic and cook over a low heat, stirring occasionally, for 6–8 minutes, until softened.

2 Increase the heat to medium, add the beans, pour in the stock and bring to the boil. Reduce the heat, cover and simmer for 2–2½ hours, until the beans are tender.

3 Remove the pan from the heat and leave to cool slightly. Ladle all or half the soup, depending on the texture you require, into a food processor or blender, and process to a purée.

4 Return the soup to the pan and bring just to the boil. If it is very thick, add a little more stock or water. Stir in the cayenne pepper, lemon juice, vinegar, sherry and hard-boiled eggs and season to taste with salt and pepper. Reduce the heat and simmer, stirring constantly, for 10 minutes.

5 Remove the pan from the heat and ladle the soup into warmed bowls. Garnish with celery leaves and serve immediately, sprinkled with grated Cheddar cheese.

traditional bean & cabbage soup

serves 6

- 200 g/7 oz dried cannellini beans, soaked overnight and drained
- 3 tbsp olive oil
- 2 red onions, roughly chopped
- 4 carrots, sliced
- 4 celery sticks, roughly chopped
- 4 garlic cloves, roughly chopped
- 600 ml/1 pint vegetable stock
- 400 g/14 oz canned chopped tomatoes
- 2 tbsp chopped fresh flat-leaf parsley
- 500 g/1 lb 2 oz cavolo nero, or Savoy cabbage trimmed and thinly sliced
- 1 small two-day-old ciabatta loaf, torn into small pieces
- salt and pepper
- extra virgin olive oil, to serve

1 Place the beans in a large saucepan. Cover with cold water and bring to the boil, skimming off any scum. Reduce the heat and simmer, uncovered, for 1–1½ hours, until tender.

2 Meanwhile, heat the olive oil in a large saucepan, add the onions, carrots and celery and cook over a medium heat for 10–15 minutes, until softened. Add the garlic and cook for 1–2 minutes.

3 Drain the beans, reserving the cooking water, and add half the beans to the pan. Add the stock, tomatoes and parsley. Season to taste with salt and pepper.

4 Bring to a simmer and cook, uncovered and stirring occasionally, for 30 minutes. Add the cavolo nero and cook, stirring occasionally, for a further 15 minutes.

5 Put the remaining beans in a food processor or blender with a little of the reserved cooking water and process to a smooth paste. Add to the soup.

6 Stir in the bread and add a little more water, if needed. The consistency should be thick. Serve immediately, drizzled with a little olive oil.

tuscan bean soup

serves 6

- 300 g/10½ oz canned cannellini beans, drained and rinsed
- 300 g/10½ oz canned borlotti beans, drained and rinsed
- 600 ml/1 pint chicken or vegetable stock
- 115 g/4 oz dried conchigliette or other small pasta shapes
- 3 tbsp olive oil, plus extra for drizzling
- 2 garlic cloves, finely chopped
- 3 tbsp chopped fresh flat-leaf parsley
- salt and pepper

1 Place half the cannellini beans and half the borlotti beans in a food processor with half the stock and process until smooth. Pour into a large, heavy-based saucepan and add the remaining beans. Stir in enough of the remaining stock to achieve the consistency you like, then bring to the boil.

2 Add the pasta and return to the boil, then reduce the heat and cook for 15 minutes, or until just tender.

3 Meanwhile, heat the oil in a small frying pan. Add the garlic and cook, stirring constantly, for 2–3 minutes, or until golden. Stir the garlic into the soup with the parsley.

4 Season to taste with salt and pepper and ladle into warmed soup bowls. Drizzle with the remaining oil to taste and serve immediately.

squash & lentil soup

serves 6

- 3 tbsp olive oil
- 2 large onions, chopped
- 2 garlic cloves, chopped
- 2 tsp ground cumin
- 1 tsp ground cinnamon
- ½ tsp freshly grated nutmeg
- ½ tsp ground ginger
- ½ tsp ground coriander
- 1 kg/2 lb 4 oz pumpkin or butternut squash, deseeded and cut into small chunks
- 350 g/12 oz red or yellow lentils
- 1.7 litres/3 pints vegetable stock
- 3 tbsp lemon juice
- salt and pepper
- crème fraîche or Greek-style yogurt, to garnish

1 Heat the oil in a large saucepan. Add the onions and garlic and cook over a low heat, stirring occasionally, for 5 minutes, until softened. Add the cumin, cinnamon, nutmeg, ginger and coriander and cook, stirring constantly, for 1 minute.

2 Stir in the pumpkin and lentils and cook, stirring constantly for 2 minutes, then pour in the stock and bring to the boil over a medium heat. Reduce the heat and simmer, stirring occasionally, for 50–60 minutes, until the vegetables are tender.

3 Remove from the heat and leave to cool slightly, then ladle into a food processor or blender, in batches if necessary, and process to a smooth purée.

4 Return the soup to the rinsed-out pan, stir in the lemon juice, season to taste with salt and pepper and reheat gently. Ladle into warmed bowls, top with a swirl of crème fraîche and serve immediately.

gazpacho

serves 4

- 1 red pepper, cored, deseeded and chopped
- 1 kg/2 lb 4 oz ripe tomatoes, cored and chopped
- 2 tbsp very finely chopped onion
- 3 garlic cloves, crushed
- 1 cucumber, peeled and chopped
- 100 g/3½ oz stale bread, crumbled
- 3 tbsp red wine vinegar or sherry vinegar
- 3½ tbsp olive oil, plus extra for drizzling
- 200 g/7 oz ice cubes (optional)
- salt and pepper

1 Set aside a handful of the red pepper, a handful of the tomatoes and half the chopped onion in the refrigerator. Put the rest in a food processor with the garlic and cucumber and puree until smooth. Add the bread, vinegar and oil and process again. Season to taste with salt and pepper. If the soup is too thick, add the ice, then place in the refrigerator for 2 hours.

2 When ready to serve, check the vinegar and seasoning. Scatter over the reserved red pepper, tomatoes and onions, then drizzle over a swirl of olive oil. Serve immediately.

french onion soup

serves 6

- 3 tbsp olive oil
- 675 g/1 lb 8 oz onions, thinly sliced
- 4 garlic cloves, 3 chopped and 1 halved
- 1 tsp sugar
- 2 tsp chopped fresh thyme, plus extra sprigs to garnish
- 2 tbsp plain flour
- 125 ml/4 fl oz dry white wine
- 2 litres/3½ pints vegetable stock
- 6 slices French bread
- 300 g/10½ oz Gruyère cheese, grated

1 Heat the oil in a large, heavy-based saucepan over a medium–low heat, add the onions and cook, stirring occasionally, for 10 minutes, or until they are just beginning to brown. Stir in the chopped garlic, sugar and chopped thyme, then reduce the heat and cook, stirring occasionally, for 30 minutes, or until the onions are golden brown.

2 Sprinkle in the flour and cook, stirring constantly, for 1–2 minutes. Stir in the wine. Gradually stir in the stock and bring to the boil, skimming off any scum that rises to the surface, then reduce the heat and simmer for 45 minutes.

3 Meanwhile, preheat the grill to medium. Toast the bread on both sides under the grill, then rub the toast with the cut edges of the halved garlic clove.

4 Ladle the soup into 6 flameproof bowls set on a baking tray. Float a piece of toast in each bowl and divide the grated cheese between them. Place under the grill for 2–3 minutes, or until the cheese has just melted. Garnish with thyme sprigs and serve immediately.

green vegetable soup

serves 6

- 1.5 litres/2¾ pints vegetable stock
- 3 tbsp olive oil
- 2 leeks, white parts only, chopped
- 2 tbsp plain flour
- 1 tsp dried thyme
- ½ tsp fennel seeds
- 1 Little Gem lettuce, roughly chopped
- 500 g/1 lb 2 oz spinach, coarse stalks removed
- 280 g/10 oz shelled fresh or frozen peas
- 1 bunch of watercress or rocket
- 4 tbsp chopped fresh mint
- salt and pepper
- 2 tbsp chopped fresh flat-leaf parsley, to garnish
- garlic and herb bread, toasted, to serve

1 Pour the stock into a saucepan and bring to the boil. Meanwhile, heat the oil in a large saucepan. Add the leeks and cook over a low heat, stirring occasionally, for 5 minutes, until softened, then remove the pan from the heat.

2 Stir in the flour until fully incorporated, then gradually stir in the hot stock, a little at a time. Season with salt and pepper and add the thyme and fennel seeds.

3 Return the pan to the heat and bring to the boil, stirring constantly. Add the lettuce, spinach, peas, watercress and mint and bring back to the boil. Boil, stirring constantly, for 3–4 minutes, then reduce the heat, cover and simmer gently for 30 minutes.

4 Remove the soup from the heat and leave to cool slightly. Ladle it into a food processor or blender, in batches if necessary, and process to a smooth purée. Return the soup to the rinsed-out pan and reheat, stirring occasionally. When it is piping hot, ladle into warmed bowls, sprinkle with the parsley and serve with garlic and herb bread.

cream of pea soup

serves 4

- 115 g/4 oz butter
- 1 onion, finely chopped
- 450 g/1 lb shelled peas
- 150 ml/5 fl oz water
- 600–700 ml/1–1¼ pints milk
- salt and pepper

1 Melt the butter in a saucepan over a low heat. Add the onion and cook, stirring occasionally, for 5 minutes, until softened.

2 Add the peas and pour in the water. Increase the heat to medium and simmer for 3–4 minutes, or until the peas are tender. (Frozen peas will be ready in 10 minutes.)

3 Add 600 ml/1 pint of the milk, season with salt and pepper and then bring to the boil, stirring constantly.

4 Remove the pan from the heat and leave to cool slightly, then pour the soup into a food processor or blender and process to a smooth purée.

5 Return the soup to the rinsed-out pan and bring back to the boil. If the soup seems too thick, heat the remaining milk in a small saucepan and stir it into the soup. Taste and adjust the seasoning if necessary, and serve.

watercress soup

serves 4

- 2 bunches of watercress (about 200 g/7 oz), thoroughly cleaned
- 40 g/1½ oz butter
- 2 onions, chopped
- 225 g/8 oz potatoes, roughly chopped
- 1.2 litres/2 pints vegetable stock or water
- whole nutmeg, for grating (optional)
- salt and pepper
- 125 ml/4 fl oz crème fraîche, to serve

1 Remove the leaves from the stalks of the watercress and set aside. Roughly chop the stalks.

2 Melt the butter in a large saucepan over a medium heat, add the onions and cook for 4–5 minutes, until soft. Do not brown.

3 Add the potatoes to the saucepan and mix well with the onions. Add the watercress stalks and the stock.

4 Bring to the boil, then reduce the heat, cover and simmer for 15–20 minutes, until the potato is soft.

5 Add the watercress leaves and stir in to heat through. Remove from the heat and transfer to a food processor or blender. Process until smooth and return the soup to the rinsed-out saucepan. Reheat and season with salt and pepper to taste, adding a good grating of nutmeg, if using.

6 Serve in warmed bowls with the crème fraîche spooned on top and an extra grating of nutmeg, if desired.

asparagus soup

serves 4

- 425 g/15 oz canned asparagus spears
- 25 g/1 oz butter
- 2 tbsp plain flour
- 600 ml/1 pint milk
- salt and pepper

1 Drain the asparagus, reserving the can juices. Cut the asparagus spears into short lengths and set aside.

2 Melt the butter in a saucepan over a low heat. Stir in the flour and cook, stirring constantly, for 1 minute. Remove the pan from the heat.

3 Gradually stir in the reserved can juices, then slowly stir in the milk. Return the pan to the heat and bring to the boil, stirring constantly. Add the asparagus spears and heat through gently for 2–3 minutes.

4 Ladle the soup into a food processor or blender, in batches if necessary, and process until smooth. Stir well before ladling into bowls. Season with pepper, and salt if necessary, and serve.

mushroom soup

serves 6

- 140 g/5 oz ciabatta or other rustic bread, crusts removed
- 55 g/2 oz butter
- 1 small onion, chopped
- 650 g/1 lb 7 oz field mushrooms, roughly chopped
- 1 garlic clove, finely chopped
- ½ tsp dried thyme
- 150 ml/5 fl oz red wine or Madeira
- 1 litre/1¾ pints vegetable stock
- salt and pepper

1 Tear the bread into pieces and put it into a bowl. Pour in cold water to cover and leave to soak for 10 minutes, then drain and squeeze out.

2 Meanwhile, melt the butter in a large saucepan. Add the onion and cook over a low heat, stirring occasionally, for 8–10 minutes, until golden. Add the mushrooms and garlic and cook, stirring frequently, for 5–7 minutes, until they have released their liquid.

3 Add the bread and thyme and pour in the wine. Cook for 2 minutes, until the alcohol has evaporated, then pour in the stock and bring to the boil over a medium heat. Reduce the heat, cover and simmer for 20–25 minutes.

4 Remove the pan from the heat and leave to cool slightly. Transfer the soup to a food processor or blender, in batches if necessary, and process to a purée.

5 Return the soup to the rinsed-out pan, season to taste with salt and pepper and reheat gently, stirring occasionally. Ladle into warmed bowls and serve.

leek & potato soup

serves 4–6
- 55 g/2 oz butter
- 1 onion, chopped
- 3 leeks, sliced
- 225 g/8 oz potatoes, cut into 2-cm/¾-inch cubes
- 850 ml/1½ pints vegetable stock
- salt and pepper
- 2 tbsp snipped fresh chives, to garnish
- 150 ml/5 fl oz single cream, to serve (optional)

1 Melt the butter in a large saucepan over a medium heat, add the onion, leeks and potatoes and sauté gently for 2–3 minutes, until soft but not brown. Pour in the stock, bring to the boil, then reduce the heat and simmer, covered, for 15 minutes.

2 Transfer the mixture to a food processor or blender and process until smooth. Return to the rinsed-out saucepan.

3 Heat the soup, season with salt and pepper to taste and serve in warmed soup bowls, garnished with chives and swirled with the cream, if using.

potato & pasta soup with pesto

serves 4
- 450 g/1 lb floury potatoes
- 3 slices pancetta, chopped
- 2 tbsp olive oil
- 450 g/1 lb onions, finely chopped
- 600 ml/1 pint chicken stock
- 600 ml/1 pint milk
- 100 g/3½ oz dried conchigliette
- 150 ml/5 fl oz double cream
- 2 tbsp chopped fresh flat-leaf parsley
- salt and pepper
- Parmesan cheese shavings, to serve

pesto
- 55 g/2 oz fresh flat-leaf parsley leaves
- 2 garlic cloves, chopped
- 55 g/2 oz pine kernels
- 2 tbsp chopped fresh basil leaves
- 55 g/2 oz Parmesan cheese, grated
- 150 ml/5 fl oz olive oil

1 To make the pesto, put all of the ingredients in a food processor or blender and process for 2 minutes, or blend by hand using a mortar and pestle.

2 Peel the potatoes and finely chop.

3 Cook the pancetta in a large saucepan over a medium heat for 4 minutes. Add the oil, potatoes and onions and cook, stirring constantly, for 12 minutes.

4 Add the stock and milk to the pan, bring to the boil and simmer for 10 minutes.

5 Add the pasta and simmer for a further 10–12 minutes.

6 Stir in the cream and simmer for 5 minutes. Add the chopped parsley and 2 tablespoons of the pesto. Season to taste with salt and pepper.

7 Ladle the soup into serving bowls and serve with Parmesan shavings.

sweet potato & stilton soup

serves 4

- 4 tbsp butter
- 1 large onion, chopped
- 2 leeks, trimmed and sliced
- 175 g/6 oz sweet potatoes, peeled and diced
- 850 ml/1½ pints vegetable stock
- 1 tbsp chopped fresh parsley
- 1 bay leaf
- 150 ml/5 fl oz double cream
- 150 g/5½ oz Stilton cheese, crumbled
- pepper
- 2 tbsp finely crumbled Stilton cheese, to garnish
- slices of fresh bread, to serve

1 Melt the butter in a large saucepan over a medium heat. Add the onion and leeks and cook, stirring, for about 3 minutes, until slightly softened. Add the sweet potatoes and cook for a further 5 minutes, stirring, then pour in the stock, add the parsley and bay leaf and season with pepper. Bring to the boil, then lower the heat, cover the pan and simmer for about 30 minutes. Remove from the heat and leave to cool for 10 minutes. Remove the bay leaf.

2 Transfer half of the soup into a food processor and blend until smooth. Return to the pan with the rest of the soup, stir in the cream and cook for a further 5 minutes. Gradually stir in the crumbled Stilton until melted (do not let the soup boil).

3 Remove from the heat and ladle into serving bowls. Garnish with finely crumbled Stilton and serve with slices of fresh bread.

broccoli & stilton soup

serves 6

- 40 g/1½ oz butter
- 2 white onions, chopped
- 1 large potato, chopped
- 750 g/1 lb 10 oz broccoli, cut into small florets
- 1.5 litres/2¾ pints vegetable stock
- 150 g/5½ oz Stilton cheese, diced
- pinch of ground mace
- salt and pepper
- croûtons, to garnish (see page 9)

1 Melt the butter in a large saucepan. Add the onions and potato and stir well. Cover and cook over a low heat for 7 minutes. Add the broccoli and stir well, then re-cover the pan and cook for a further 5 minutes.

2 Increase the heat to medium, pour in the stock and bring to the boil. Reduce the heat, season with salt and pepper, re-cover and simmer for 15–20 minutes, until the vegetables are tender.

3 Remove the pan from the heat, strain into a bowl, reserving the vegetables, and leave to cool slightly. Put the vegetables into a food processor or blender, add 1 ladleful of the stock and process to a smooth purée. With the motor running, gradually add the remaining stock.

4 Return the soup to the rinsed-out pan and reheat gently, but do not allow the soup to boil. Remove from the heat and stir in the cheese until melted and thoroughly combined. Stir in the mace and taste and adjust the seasoning, if necessary. Ladle into warmed bowls, sprinkle with the croûtons and serve immediately.

spinach & cheese soup

serves 6–8

- 225 g/8 oz fresh baby spinach leaves, tough stalks removed
- 600 ml/1 pint milk
- 700 ml/1¼ pints vegetable or chicken stock
- 200 g/7 oz Boursin or other cream cheese flavoured with garlic and herbs
- salt and pepper
- croûtons, to garnish (see page 9)

1 Put the spinach in a large saucepan and pour in the milk and stock. Bring to the boil, then reduce the heat and simmer gently for 12 minutes. Remove the pan from the heat and leave to cool completely.

2 Ladle the cold soup into a food processor or blender, in batches if necessary, and process until smooth. Cut the cheese into chunks and add to the soup. Process again until smooth and creamy.

3 Pour the soup into a bowl and season to taste with salt and pepper. Cover with clingfilm and leave to chill in the refrigerator for at least 3 hours. Stir well before ladling into bowls. Add the croutons and serve immediately.

miso soup

serves 4

- 1 litre/1¾ pints water
- 2 tsp dashi granules
- 175 g/6 oz silken tofu, drained and cut into small cubes
- 4 shiitake mushrooms or white mushrooms, finely sliced
- 4 tbsp miso paste
- 2 spring onions, chopped

1 Put the water in a large pan with the dashi granules and bring to a boil.

2 Add the tofu and mushrooms, reduce the heat, and simmer for 3 minutes.

3 Stir in the miso paste and simmer gently, stirring, until it has dissolved.

4 Add the spring onions and serve immediately.

5 The miso paste will begin to settle, so stir the soup before serving to recombine.

hot & sour soup tom yum

serves 4

- 2 fresh red chillies, deseeded and roughly chopped
- 6 tbsp rice vinegar
- 1.2 litres/2 pints vegetable stock
- 2 lemon grass stalks, halved
- 4 tbsp soy sauce
- 1 tbsp palm sugar
- juice of ½ lime
- 2 tbsp groundnut or vegetable oil
- 225 g/8 oz firm tofu (drained weight), cut into 1-cm/½-inch cubes
- 400 g/14 oz canned straw mushrooms, drained
- 4 spring onions, chopped
- 1 small head pak choi, shredded

1 Mix the chillies and vinegar together in a non-metallic bowl, cover and leave to stand at room temperature for 1 hour.

2 Meanwhile, bring the stock to the boil in a saucepan. Add the lemon grass, soy sauce, sugar and lime juice, reduce the heat and simmer for 20–30 minutes.

3 Heat the oil in a preheated wok, add the tofu cubes and stir-fry over a high heat for 2–3 minutes, or until browned all over. (You may need to do this in 2 batches, depending on the size of the wok.)

4 Remove with a slotted spoon and drain on kitchen paper.

5 Add the chillies and vinegar with the tofu, mushrooms and half the spring onions to the stock mixture and cook for 10 minutes.

6 Mix the remaining spring onions with the pak choi and scatter over the soup before serving.

mushroom & ginger soup

serves 4

- 15 g/½ oz dried Chinese mushrooms
- 1 litre/1¾ pints vegetable stock
- 125 g/4½ oz thread egg noodles
- 2 tsp sunflower oil
- 3 garlic cloves, crushed
- 2.5-cm/1-inch piece fresh ginger, finely shredded
- ½ tsp mushroom ketchup
- 1 tsp light soy sauce
- 125 g/4½ oz beansprouts
- fresh coriander sprigs, to garnish

1 Soak the dried Chinese mushrooms for at least 30 minutes in 300 ml/10 fl oz of the hot stock. Drain the mushrooms and reserve the stock. Remove the stalks of the mushrooms and discard. Slice the caps and reserve.

2 Cook the noodles according to the instructions on the packet. Drain well, rinse under cold water, and drain again. Set aside.

3 Heat the oil in a preheated wok or large frying pan over a high heat. Add the garlic and ginger, stir and add the mushrooms. Stir over a high heat for 2 minutes.

4 Add the remaining stock with the reserved stock and bring to the boil. Add the mushroom ketchup and soy sauce. Stir in the beansprouts and cook until tender.

5 Place some noodles in each soup bowl and ladle the soup on top. Garnish with fresh coriander sprigs and serve immediately.

Mmmm... meat

beef & tomato soup

serves 6

- 3 tbsp sunflower oil
- 1 onion, finely chopped
- 1 garlic clove, finely chopped
- 2 fresh red chillies, deseeded and finely chopped
- 4 large tomatoes, peeled and chopped
- 500 g/1 lb 2 oz fresh beef mince
- 2 carrots, diced
- 2 potatoes, diced
- 1–2 tbsp chopped fresh flat-leaf parsley, plus extra to garnish
- 1.2 litres/2 pints beef stock
- salt and pepper
- crusty rolls, to serve

1 Heat the oil in a large saucepan. Add the onion and garlic and cook over a low heat, stirring occasionally, for 5 minutes, until softened. Stir in the chillies and tomatoes and cook for a further 5 minutes. Add the beef, increase the heat to medium and cook, breaking it up with a wooden spoon, for 6–8 minutes, until lightly browned.

2 Stir in the carrots, potatoes and parsley, pour in the stock and season to taste with salt and pepper. Bring to the boil, then reduce the heat, cover and simmer for 30 minutes, until the meat and vegetables are tender.

3 Taste and adjust the seasoning, adding salt and pepper if needed. Ladle the soup into warmed bowls, garnish with parsley and serve immediately with crusty rolls.

beef & vegetable soup

serves 4

- 55 g/2 oz pearl barley
- 1.2 litres/2 pints beef stock
- 1 tsp dried mixed herbs
- 225 g/8 oz lean rump or sirloin beef
- 1 large carrot, diced
- 1 leek, shredded
- 1 medium onion, chopped
- 2 celery sticks, sliced
- salt and pepper
- 2 tbsp chopped fresh parsley, to garnish

1 Place the pearl barley in a large saucepan. Pour over the stock and add the mixed herbs. Bring to the boil, cover and simmer gently over a low heat for 10 minutes.

2 Meanwhile, trim any fat from the beef and cut the meat into thin strips.

3 Skim away any scum that has risen to the top of the stock with a flat ladle.

4 Add the beef, carrot, leek, onion and celery to the pan. Bring back to the boil, cover and simmer for about 1 hour, or until the pearl barley, beef and vegetables are just tender.

5 Skim away any remaining scum that has risen to the top of the soup with a flat ladle. Blot the surface with absorbent kitchen paper to remove any fat. Adjust the seasoning according to taste.

6 Ladle the soup into warmed bowls, garnish with chopped parsley and serve hot.

beef mince & coriander soup

serves 4–6

- 225 g/8 oz beef mince
- 1.7 litres/3 pints chicken stock
- 3 egg whites, lightly beaten
- 1 tsp salt
- ½ tsp white pepper
- 1 tbsp finely chopped fresh ginger
- 1 tbsp finely chopped spring onion
- 4–5 tbsp finely chopped coriander, tough stems removed

marinade

- 1 tsp salt
- 1 tsp sugar
- 1 tsp Shaoxing rice wine
- 1 tsp light soy sauce

1 Combine all the ingredients for the marinade in a bowl and add the beef. Allow to marinate for 20 minutes.

2 Bring the stock to the boil in a large saucepan. Add the beef, stirring to break up any clumps, and simmer for 10 minutes.

3 Slowly add the egg whites, stirring rapidly so that they form into fine shreds. Add the salt and pepper and taste to check the seasoning.

4 To serve, place the ginger, spring onion and coriander in the base of each individual bowl and pour the soup on top.

beef & bean soup

serves 4
- 2 tbsp vegetable oil
- 1 large onion, finely chopped
- 2 garlic cloves, finely chopped
- 1 green pepper, deseeded and sliced
- 2 carrots, sliced
- 400 g/14 oz canned black-eye beans
- 225 g/8 oz fresh beef mince
- 1 tsp each ground cumin, chilli powder and paprika
- ¼ cabbage, sliced
- 225 g/8 oz tomatoes, peeled and chopped
- 600 ml/1 pint beef stock
- salt and pepper

1 Heat the oil in a large saucepan over a medium heat. Add the onion and garlic and cook, stirring frequently, for 5 minutes, or until softened. Add the pepper and carrots and cook for a further 5 minutes.

2 Meanwhile, drain the beans, reserving the liquid from the can. Place two thirds of the beans, reserving the remainder, in a food processor or blender with the bean liquid and process until smooth.

3 Add the beef to the saucepan and cook, stirring constantly, to break up any lumps, until well browned. Add the spices and cook, stirring, for 2 minutes. Add the cabbage, tomatoes, stock and puréed beans and season to taste with salt and pepper. Bring to the boil, then reduce the heat, cover and simmer for 15 minutes, or until the vegetables are tender.

4 Stir in the reserved beans, cover and simmer for a further 5 minutes. Ladle the soup into warmed soup bowls and serve.

meat-in-a-bowl beef & herb soup

serves 6

- 2 onions
- 2 tbsp sunflower oil
- 1 tbsp ground turmeric
- 1 tsp ground cumin
- 100 g/3½ oz green or yellow split peas
- 1.2 litres/2 pints beef stock
- 225 g/8 oz fresh beef mince
- 200 g/7 oz long-grain rice
- 1 tbsp chopped fresh coriander
- 1 tbsp snipped fresh chives
- 55 g/2 oz baby spinach, finely chopped
- 25 g/1 oz butter
- 2 garlic cloves, finely chopped
- 3 tbsp chopped fresh mint
- salt and pepper
- Greek-style yogurt, to serve

1 Grate one of the onions into a bowl and finely chop the other. Heat the oil in a large saucepan. Add the chopped onion and cook over a low–medium heat, stirring occasionally, for 8–10 minutes, until golden. Stir in the turmeric and cumin, add the split peas and pour in the stock. Bring to the boil, then reduce the heat, cover and simmer for 15 minutes.

2 Meanwhile, add the beef to the grated onion, season to taste with salt and pepper and mix well. Shape the mixture into small balls.

3 Add the meatballs to the soup, re-cover the pan and simmer for a further 10 minutes. Add the rice and stir in the coriander, chives and spinach. Simmer, stirring frequently, for 25–30 minutes, until the rice is tender.

4 Melt the butter in a frying pan. Add the garlic and cook over a low heat, stirring frequently, for 2–3 minutes. Stir in the mint and cook for a further minute.

5 Transfer the soup to warmed bowls and sprinkle over the garlic mixture. Serve immediately with Greek-style yogurt.

beef goulash soup

serves 6
- 1 tbsp oil
- 500 g/1 lb 2 oz fresh lean beef mince
- 2 onions, finely chopped
- 2 garlic cloves, finely chopped
- 2 tbsp plain flour
- 225 ml/8 fl oz water
- 400 g/14 oz canned chopped tomatoes
- 1 carrot, finely chopped
- 225 g/8 oz red pepper, roasted, peeled, deseeded and chopped
- 1 tsp Hungarian paprika
- ¼ tsp caraway seeds
- pinch of dried oregano
- 1 litre/1¾ pints beef stock
- 55 g/2 oz tagliatelle, broken into small pieces
- salt and pepper
- soured cream and sprigs of fresh coriander, to garnish

1 Heat the oil in a large wide saucepan over a medium–high heat. Add the beef and sprinkle with salt and pepper. Fry until lightly browned.

2 Reduce the heat and add the onions and garlic. Cook for about 3 minutes, stirring frequently, until the onions are softened. Stir in the flour and continue cooking for 1 minute.

3 Add the water and stir to combine well, scraping the bottom of the pan to mix in the flour. Stir in the tomatoes, carrot, pepper, paprika, caraway seeds, oregano and stock.

4 Bring just to the boil. Reduce the heat, cover and simmer gently for about 40 minutes, stirring occasionally, until all the vegetables are tender.

5 Add the tagliatelle to the soup and simmer for a further 20 minutes, or until the tagliatelle is cooked.

6 Taste the soup and adjust the seasoning, if necessary. Ladle into warmed bowls and top each with a tablespoonful of soured cream. Garnish with coriander and serve.

vietnamese beef soup

serves 2

- 1.2 litres/2 pints beef stock
- 1 small fresh chilli, chopped
- 1 cinnamon stick
- 2 star anise
- 2 cloves
- 225 g/8 oz sirloin or fillet steak, cut into thin strips
- 300 g/10½ oz rice noodles
- 4 tbsp chopped fresh coriander
- lime wedges, to garnish

1 Heat the stock, chilli and spices in a saucepan until boiling, then reduce the heat and simmer for about 5 minutes.

2 Add the beef strips and simmer for a further 2–3 minutes, until cooked to your liking.

3 Cook the noodles according to the packet instructions, then drain and place in 2 serving bowls.

4 Pour over the broth and sprinkle with chopped coriander. Garnish with lime wedges and serve immediately.

chinese soup with meatballs

serves 4–6

- 5 dried Chinese mushrooms
- 350 g/12 oz fresh beef mince
- 1 onion, finely chopped
- 1 garlic clove, finely chopped
- 1 tbsp cornflour
- 1 egg, lightly beaten
- 850 ml/1½ pints beef stock
- 1 bunch of watercress (about 25 g/1 oz), stalks removed
- 3 spring onions, finely chopped
- 1–1½ tbsp soy sauce

1 Put the mushrooms into a bowl and pour in warm water to cover. Leave to soak for 15 minutes, then drain and squeeze dry. Discard the stalks and thinly slice the caps.

2 Mix together the beef, onion, garlic, cornflour and egg in a bowl until thoroughly combined. Shape the mixture into small balls, drop them into a bowl of iced water and leave to stand for 15 minutes.

3 Pour the stock into a large saucepan and bring to the boil. Drain the meatballs well, add to the pan and bring back to the boil. Reduce the heat and simmer for 10 minutes. Add the mushrooms, watercress, spring onions and soy sauce to taste and simmer for a further 2 minutes. Serve immediately.

spicy beef & noodle soup

serves 4

- 1 litre/1¾ pints beef stock
- 150 ml/5 fl oz vegetable or groundnut oil
- 85 g/3 oz rice vermicelli noodles
- 2 shallots, thinly sliced
- 2 garlic cloves, crushed
- 2.5-cm/1-inch piece fresh ginger, thinly sliced
- 225 g/8 oz fillet steak, cut into thin strips
- 2 tbsp green curry paste
- 2 tbsp Thai soy sauce
- 1 tbsp nam pla (fish sauce)
- chopped fresh coriander, to garnish

1 Pour the stock into a large saucepan and bring to the boil. Meanwhile, heat the oil in a wok or large frying pan. Add a third of the noodles and fry for 10–20 seconds, until they have puffed up. Lift out with tongs, drain on kitchen paper and set aside. Discard all but 2 tablespoons of the oil.

2 Add the shallots, garlic and ginger to the wok and stir-fry for 1 minute. Add the beef and curry paste and stir-fry for a further 3–4 minutes, until tender.

3 Add the beef mixture, the uncooked noodles, soy sauce and nam pla to the saucepan of stock and simmer for 2–3 minutes, until the noodles have swelled. Serve hot, garnished with the chopped coriander and the reserved crispy noodles.

mexican-style beef & rice soup

serves 4

- 3 tbsp olive oil
- 500 g/1 lb 2 oz boneless stewing beef, cut into 2.5-cm/1-inch pieces
- 150 ml/5 fl oz red wine
- 1 onion, finely chopped
- 1 green pepper, deseeded and finely chopped
- 1 small fresh red chilli, deseeded and finely chopped
- 2 garlic cloves, finely chopped
- 1 carrot, finely chopped
- ¼ tsp ground coriander
- ¼ tsp ground cumin
- ⅛ tsp ground cinnamon
- ¼ tsp dried oregano
- 1 bay leaf
- grated rind of ½ orange
- 400 g/14 oz canned chopped tomatoes
- 1.2 litres/2 pints beef stock
- 50 g/1¾ oz long-grain white rice
- 25 g/1 oz raisins
- 15 g/½ oz plain chocolate, melted
- chopped fresh coriander, to garnish

1 Heat half the oil in a large frying pan over a medium–high heat. Add the meat in one layer and cook until well browned, turning to colour all sides. Remove the pan from the heat and pour in the wine.

2 Heat the remaining oil in a large saucepan over a medium heat. Add the onion, cover and cook for about 3 minutes, stirring occasionally, until just softened. Add the green pepper, chilli, garlic and carrot, and continue cooking, covered, for 3 minutes.

3 Add the coriander, cumin, cinnamon, oregano, bay leaf and orange rind. Stir in the tomatoes and stock, along with the beef and wine. Bring almost to the boil and when the mixture begins to bubble, reduce the heat to low. Cover and simmer gently, stirring occasionally, for about 1 hour until the meat is tender.

4 Stir in the rice, raisins and chocolate, and continue cooking, stirring occasionally, for about 30 minutes until the rice is tender. Remove from the heat and discard the bay leaf.

5 Ladle into warmed bowls and garnish with coriander.

taco soup

serves 4–6

- 1 tbsp sunflower oil
- 1 small onion, finely chopped
- 225 g/8 oz fresh beef mince
- 400 g/14 oz canned chopped tomatoes
- 400 g/14 oz canned red kidney beans
- 225 ml/8 fl oz tomato juice
- 1 tsp sugar
- ¼ tsp ground cinnamon
- ¼ tsp ground cumin
- 1 tsp chilli powder
- 350 ml/12 fl oz beef stock
- 115 g/4 oz Cheddar cheese, coarsely grated
- 350 g/12 oz tortilla chips
- 225 ml/8 fl oz soured cream
- 1 avocado
- 2 tbsp lemon juice

1 Heat the oil in a large saucepan. Add the onion and cook over a low heat, stirring occasionally, for 5 minutes, until softened. Add the beef, increase the heat to medium and cook, stirring frequently and breaking it up with a wooden spoon, for 8–10 minutes. Drain off as much fat as possible.

2 Stir in the tomatoes, kidney beans with their can juices, tomato juice, sugar, spices and stock and bring to the boil. Reduce the heat, cover and simmer, stirring occasionally, for 15 minutes.

3 Meanwhile, put the cheese, tortilla chips and soured cream into separate serving dishes. Peel, stone and dice the avocado and gently toss with the lemon juice in a bowl.

4 Remove the soup from the heat and ladle into warmed soup bowls. Scatter the avocado over the soup and serve immediately with the cheese, tortilla chips and soured cream.

pork & vegetable broth

serves 4
- 1 tbsp chilli oil
- 1 garlic clove, chopped
- 3 spring onions, sliced
- 1 red pepper, deseeded and finely sliced
- 2 tbsp cornflour
- 1 litre/1¾ pints vegetable stock
- 1 tbsp soy sauce
- 2 tbsp rice wine or dry sherry
- 150 g/5½ oz pork fillet, sliced
- 1 tbsp finely chopped lemon grass
- 1 small red chilli, deseeded and finely chopped
- 1 tbsp grated fresh ginger
- 115 g/4 oz fine egg noodles
- 200 g/7 oz canned water chestnuts, drained and sliced
- salt and pepper

1 Heat the oil in a large saucepan. Add the garlic and spring onions and cook over a medium heat, stirring, for 3 minutes, until slightly softened. Add the red pepper and cook for a further 5 minutes, stirring.

2 In a bowl, mix the cornflour with enough of the stock to make a smooth paste, then stir it into the pan. Cook, stirring, for 2 minutes. Stir in the remaining stock and the soy sauce and rice wine, then add the pork, lemon grass, chilli and ginger. Season with salt and pepper. Bring to the boil, then lower the heat and simmer for 25 minutes.

3 Bring a separate saucepan of water to the boil, add the noodles and cook for 3 minutes. Remove from the heat, drain, then add the noodles to the soup along with the water chestnuts. Cook for a further 2 minutes, then remove from the heat and ladle into serving bowls.

salt pork & lentil soup

serves 6-8

- 225 g/8 oz salt pork, diced
- 2 tbsp olive oil
- 1 onion, chopped
- 3 garlic cloves, finely chopped
- 4 potatoes, diced
- 500 g/1 lb 2 oz red lentils
- 2 litres/3½ pints vegetable stock
- 1 bouquet garni (1 bay leaf, 1 fresh thyme sprig and 3 fresh parsley sprigs, tied together)
- salt and pepper
- crusty bread, to serve

1 Put the salt pork into a large saucepan and cook over medium heat, stirring frequently, for 8–10 minutes, until it has released most of its fat and is browned all over. Remove from the pan with a slotted spoon and drain on kitchen paper. Set aside.

2 Add the oil to the pan and heat. Add the onion, garlic and potatoes and cook over a low heat, stirring occasionally, for 5 minutes, until the onion has softened. Stir in the lentils and cook, stirring constantly, for 5 minutes.

3 Pour in the stock, increase the heat to medium, add the bouquet garni and bring to the boil, stirring constantly. Reduce the heat, cover and simmer for 1½–2 hours, until the lentils are very soft. Stir in the salt pork, season to taste with salt and pepper, and cook, stirring occasionally, for a further 10 minutes, until heated through.

4 Remove the pan from the heat. Remove and discard the bouquet garni. Pour the soup into warmed bowls and serve immediately with crusty bread.

split pea & ham soup

serves 6–8

- 500 g/1 lb 2 oz split green peas
- 1 tbsp olive oil
- 1 large onion, finely chopped
- 1 large carrot, finely chopped
- 1 celery stick, finely chopped
- 1 litre/1¾ pints chicken or vegetable stock
- 1 litre/1¾ pints water
- 225 g/8 oz lean smoked ham, finely diced
- ¼ tsp dried thyme
- ¼ tsp dried marjoram
- 1 bay leaf
- salt and pepper

1 Rinse the peas under cold running water. Put in a saucepan and cover generously with water. Bring to the boil and boil for 3 minutes, skimming off the scum from the surface. Drain the peas.

2 Heat the oil in a large saucepan over a medium heat. Add the onion and cook for 3–4 minutes, stirring occasionally, until just softened.

3 Add the carrot and celery and continue cooking for 2 minutes. Add the peas, pour over the stock and water and stir to combine.

4 Bring just to the boil and stir the ham into the soup. Add the thyme, marjoram and bay leaf. Reduce the heat, cover and cook gently for 1–1½ hours, until the ingredients are very soft. Remove the bay leaf.

5 Taste and adjust the seasoning. Ladle into warmed soup bowls and serve.

wonton soup

serves 6–8

- 2 litres/3½ pints chicken stock
- 2 tsp salt
- ½ tsp white pepper
- 2 tbsp finely chopped spring onion, to serve
- 1 tbsp chopped fresh coriander leaves, to serve

wontons

- 175 g/6 oz minced pork, not too lean
- 225 g/8 oz raw prawns, peeled, deveined and chopped
- ½ tsp finely chopped fresh ginger
- 1 tbsp light soy sauce
- 1 tbsp Shaoxing rice wine
- 2 tsp finely chopped spring onion
- pinch of sugar
- pinch of white pepper
- dash of sesame oil
- 30 square wonton wrappers
- 1 egg white, lightly beaten

1 For the wonton filling, mix together the pork, prawns, ginger, soy sauce, rice wine, spring onion, sugar, pepper and sesame oil, and stir well until the texture is thick and pasty. Set aside for at least 20 minutes.

2 To make the wontons, place a teaspoon of the filling at the centre of a wrapper. Brush the edges with a little egg white. Bring the opposite points towards each other and press the edges together, creating a flower-like shape. Repeat with the remaining wrappers and filling.

3 To make the soup, bring the stock to the boil and add the salt and pepper. Boil the wontons in the stock for about 5 minutes until the wrappers begin to wrinkle around the filling.

4 To serve, put the spring onion in individual bowls, spoon in the wontons and soup and top with the coriander.

pork rib soup with pickled mustard leaves

serves 6

- 1 tbsp groundnut oil
- 3 garlic cloves, thinly sliced, plus extra to garnish
- 1.2 litres/2 pints vegetable stock
- 500 g/1 lb 2 oz pork spare ribs
- 85 g/3 oz cellophane noodles
- 280 g/10 oz canned Thai pickled mustard leaves or Chinese snow pickles, well-rinsed and roughly chopped
- 2 tbsp nam pla (fish sauce)
- ½ tsp sugar
- pepper
- 1 red and 1 green chilli, deseeded and thinly sliced, to garnish

1 Heat the oil in a small frying pan or wok. Add the garlic and stir-fry for a few minutes, until golden. Transfer to a plate and set aside.

2 Pour the stock into a saucepan and bring to the boil over a medium heat. Add the spare ribs and bring back to the boil, then reduce the heat, cover and simmer for 15 minutes, until tender.

3 Meanwhile, put the cellophane noodles into a bowl, pour in hot water to cover and leave to soak for 10 minutes, until softened. Drain well.

4 Add the noodles and pickled leaves to the soup and bring back to the boil. Stir in the nam pla and sugar, season to taste with pepper and ladle into warmed bowls. Garnish with the garlic slices and red and green chillies and serve immediately.

sauerkraut & sausage soup

serves 6

- 2 tbsp butter
- 1 tbsp plain flour
- 1 tbsp sweet paprika
- 2 litres/3½ pints vegetable stock
- 650 g/1 lb 7 oz sauerkraut, drained
- 500 g/1 lb 2 oz smoked pork sausages, cut into 2.5-cm/1-inch slices
- 150 ml/5 fl oz soured cream
- salt and pepper

dumplings

- 85 g/3 oz strong white bread flour, plus extra for dusting
- pinch of salt
- 1 large egg

1 Melt the butter in a large saucepan over a low heat. Add the flour and paprika and cook, stirring constantly, for 2 minutes, then remove the pan from the heat. Gradually stir in the stock, a little at a time, until fully incorporated and the mixture is smooth.

2 Return the pan to medium heat and bring to the boil, stirring constantly. Add the sauerkraut and sausages and season with salt and pepper. Reduce the heat, cover and simmer for 30 minutes.

3 Meanwhile, make the dumplings. Sift together the flour and salt into a bowl. Beat the egg in another bowl, then gradually beat in the dry ingredients, a little at a time. Turn out on to a floured surface and knead until smooth. Cover and leave to rest for 15 minutes.

4 Divide the dough into 6 pieces and roll into sausage shapes. Flour your hands, pinch off pieces of the dough and add to the soup. Re-cover the pan and simmer for a further 5 minutes. Remove the pan from the heat, stir in the soured cream and serve immediately.

sausage & red cabbage soup

serves 4

- 2 tbsp olive oil
- 1 garlic clove, chopped
- 1 large onion, chopped
- 1 large leek, sliced
- 2 tbsp cornflour
- 1 litre/1¾ pints vegetable stock
- 450 g/1 lb potatoes, sliced
- 200 g/7 oz skinless sausages, sliced
- 150 g/5½ oz red cabbage, chopped
- 200 g/7 oz canned black-eye beans, drained
- 125 ml/4 fl oz double cream
- salt and pepper
- paprika, to garnish

1 Heat the oil in a large saucepan. Add the garlic and onion and cook over a medium heat, stirring, for 3 minutes, until slightly softened. Add the leek and cook for a further 3 minutes, stirring.

2 In a bowl, mix the cornflour with enough stock to make a smooth paste, then stir it into the pan. Cook, stirring, for 2 minutes. Stir in the remaining stock, then add the potatoes and sausages. Season with salt and pepper. Bring to the boil, then lower the heat and simmer for 25 minutes.

3 Add the red cabbage and beans and cook for 10 minutes, then stir in the cream and cook for a further 5 minutes. Remove from the heat and ladle into serving bowls. Garnish with paprika and serve immediately.

split pea & sausage soup

serves 6

- 175 g/6 oz boneless belly of pork, cut into cubes
- 2 litres/3½ pints vegetable stock
- 1 onion, chopped
- 4 leeks, chopped
- 3 carrots, chopped
- 3 celery sticks, chopped
- 1 tart eating apple, peeled, cored and chopped
- 375 g/13 oz split peas, soaked overnight in cold water to cover, drained and rinsed
- 1 bouquet garni (see page 86)
- 1 tbsp treacle
- 2 tbsp butter
- 4 bockwurst, Wienerwurst or frankfurters, cut into 2.5-cm/1-inch lengths
- salt and pepper
- crusty rye bread, to serve

1 Put the pork into a large saucepan and pour in the stock. Add the onion, leeks, carrots, celery, apple, peas, bouquet garni and treacle and bring to the boil. Using a skimmer or slotted spoon, skim off any scum that rises to the surface, then reduce the heat, cover and simmer, stirring occasionally, for 2 hours.

2 Season the soup to taste with salt and pepper and remove and discard the bouquet garni. Stir in the butter and sausages and simmer for a further 5 minutes. Serve immediately with rye bread.

cheese &
bacon soup

serves 4
- 2 tbsp butter
- 2 garlic cloves, chopped
- 1 large onion, sliced
- 250 g/9 oz smoked lean back bacon, chopped
- 2 large leeks, trimmed and sliced
- 2 tbsp plain flour
- 1 litre/1¾ pints vegetable stock
- 450 g/1 lb potatoes, chopped
- 100 ml/3½ fl oz double cream
- 300 g/10½ oz grated Cheddar cheese, plus extra to garnish
- salt and pepper

1 Melt the butter in a large saucepan over a medium heat. Add the garlic and onion and cook, stirring, for 3 minutes, until slightly softened. Add the chopped bacon and leeks and cook for a further 3 minutes, stirring.

2 In a bowl, mix the flour with enough stock to make a smooth paste, then stir it into the pan. Cook, stirring, for 2 minutes. Pour in the remaining stock, then add the potatoes. Season with salt and pepper. Bring the soup to the boil, then lower the heat and simmer gently for 25 minutes, until the potatoes are tender and cooked through.

3 Stir in the cream and cook for 5 minutes, then gradually stir in the cheese until melted. Remove from the heat and ladle into serving bowls. Garnish with grated Cheddar cheese and serve immediately.

bacon & lentil soup

serves 4
- 450 g/1 lb thick, rindless smoked bacon rashers, diced
- 1 onion, chopped
- 2 carrots, sliced
- 2 celery sticks, chopped
- 1 turnip, chopped
- 1 large potato, chopped
- 85 g/3 oz Puy lentils
- 1 bouquet garni (see page 86)
- 1 litre/1¾ pints water or chicken stock
- salt and pepper

1 Heat a large, heavy-based saucepan or flameproof casserole. Add the bacon and cook over a medium heat, stirring, for 4–5 minutes, or until the fat runs. Add the chopped onion, carrots, celery, turnip and potato and cook, stirring frequently, for 5 minutes.

2 Add the lentils and bouquet garni and pour in the water or stock. Bring to the boil, reduce the heat and simmer for 1 hour, or until the lentils are tender.

3 Remove and discard the bouquet garni and season the soup to taste with pepper, and with salt, if necessary. Ladle into warmed soup bowls and serve immediately.

brown lentil &
pasta soup

serves 4
- 4 rashers streaky bacon, cut into small squares
- 1 onion, chopped
- 2 garlic cloves, crushed
- 2 celery sticks, chopped
- 50 g/1¾ oz dried farfalline
- 400 g/14 oz canned brown lentils, drained
- 1.2 litres/2 pints vegetable stock
- 2 tbsp chopped fresh mint, plus extra sprigs to garnish

1 Place the bacon in a large frying pan together with the onion, garlic and celery. Dry-fry for 4–5 minutes, stirring, until the onion is tender and the bacon is just beginning to brown.

2 Add the pasta to the frying pan and cook, stirring, for 1 minute to coat the pasta in the fat.

3 Add the lentils and the vegetable stock and bring to the boil. Reduce the heat and leave to simmer for 12–15 minutes, or until the pasta is tender but still firm to the bite.

4 Remove the frying pan from the heat and stir in the chopped fresh mint. Transfer the soup to warmed soup bowls, garnish with fresh mint sprigs and serve immediately.

scotch broth

serves 4
- 1 tbsp vegetable oil
- 500 g/1 lb 2 oz lean neck of lamb
- 1 large onion, sliced
- 2 carrots, sliced
- 2 leeks, sliced
- 1 litre/1¾ pints vegetable stock
- 1 bay leaf
- sprigs of fresh parsley
- 55 g/2 oz pearl barley
- salt and pepper

1 Heat the vegetable oil in a large, heavy-based saucepan and add the pieces of lamb, turning them to seal and brown on both sides. Lift the lamb out of the pan and set aside until required.

2 Add the onion, carrots and leeks to the saucepan and cook gently for about 3 minutes.

3 Return the lamb to the saucepan and add the vegetable stock, bay leaf, parsley and pearl barley to the saucepan. Bring the mixture in the pan to the boil, then reduce the heat. Cover and simmer for 1½–2 hours.

4 Discard the parsley sprigs and the bay leaf. Lift the pieces of lamb from the broth and allow them to cool slightly. Remove the bones and any fat and chop the meat. Return the lamb to the broth and reheat gently. Season to taste with salt and pepper.

5 It is advisable to prepare this soup a day ahead, then leave it to cool, cover and refrigerate overnight. When ready to serve, remove and discard the layer of fat from the surface and reheat the soup gently. Ladle into warmed bowls and serve immediately.

mixed vegetable soup with lamb meatballs

serves 6

- 2 onions, finely chopped
- 1 small celeriac, diced
- ½ swede, diced
- 3 carrots, diced
- 2 potatoes, diced
- 2 red peppers, deseeded and diced
- 4 tomatoes, peeled, deseeded and chopped
- 115 g/4 oz shelled fresh or frozen peas
- 1 lemon, sliced
- 1.5 litres/2¾ pints vegetable stock
- salt and pepper

lamb meatballs

- 350 g/12 oz minced lamb
- 3 tbsp chopped fresh parsley
- 70 g/2½ oz medium-grain rice
- plain flour, for dusting
- salt and pepper

1 Put the onions, celeriac, swede, carrots, potatoes, red peppers, tomatoes, peas and lemon slices into a large saucepan, pour in the stock and season with salt and pepper. Bring to the boil, then reduce the heat, cover and simmer for 25–30 minutes.

2 Meanwhile, make the meatballs. Mix together the lamb, parsley and rice in a bowl, kneading well until thoroughly combined. Season with salt and pepper. Break off pieces of the mixture, about the size of golf balls, and shape them into balls between the palms of your hand. Dust with flour, shaking off the excess.

3 Add the meatballs to the soup, re-cover the pan and cook, stirring occasionally, for a further 40–45 minutes. Serve immediately.

chunky potato & beef soup

serves 4

- 2 tbsp vegetable oil
- 225 g/8 oz lean braising or frying steak, cut into strips
- 225 g/8 oz new potatoes, halved
- 1 carrot, diced
- 2 celery sticks, sliced
- 2 leeks, sliced
- 850 ml/1½ pints beef stock
- 8 baby sweetcorn cobs, sliced
- 1 bouquet garni (see page 86)
- 2 tbsp dry sherry
- salt and pepper
- chopped fresh flat-leaf parsley, to garnish

1 Heat the vegetable oil in a large saucepan. Add the strips of meat to the saucepan and cook for 3 minutes, turning constantly. Add the potatoes, carrot, celery and leeks to the saucepan. Cook for a further 5 minutes, stirring.

2 Pour the beef stock into the saucepan and bring to the boil. Reduce the heat until the liquid is simmering, then add the baby sweetcorn cobs and the bouquet garni. Cook for a further 20 minutes, or until cooked through.

3 Remove and discard the bouquet garni. Stir the dry sherry into the soup, then season to taste with salt and pepper.

4 Ladle the soup into warmed bowls, garnish with chopped parsley and serve.

lamb & lemon soup

serves 6
- 55 g/2 oz plain flour
- 500 g/1 lb 2 oz boneless leg of lamb, cut into cubes
- 3 tbsp olive oil
- 1.2 litres/2 pints vegetable stock
- 2 carrots, cut into chunks
- 2 onions, cut into quarters
- 1 tsp cayenne pepper
- 3 egg yolks
- 2 tbsp lemon juice
- salt and pepper
- 3 tbsp chopped fresh mint, to garnish
- flatbread, to serve

to garnish
- 55 g/2 oz butter
- ½ tsp ground cinnamon
- 2 tsp sweet or hot paprika

1 Put the flour into a plastic bag and season with salt and pepper. Add the cubes of lamb, a few at a time, seal the bag and shake to coat. Shake off any excess.

2 Heat the oil in a large saucepan. Add the lamb and cook over a medium heat, stirring frequently, for 8–10 minutes, until lightly browned all over. Pour in the stock and bring to the boil, skimming off the scum that rises to the surface.

3 Add the carrots, onions and cayenne pepper, season with salt and pepper and bring back to the boil. Reduce the heat, cover and simmer for 1½–2 hours, until the meat is tender.

4 Meanwhile, make the garnish. Melt the butter in a saucepan over a very low heat or in a microwave-safe bowl in the microwave. Remove from the heat and stir in the cinnamon and paprika.

5 Beat the egg yolks with the lemon juice in a bowl. Remove the pan from the heat and whisk a ladleful of the hot soup into the egg mixture, then add it to the pan. Return the pan to a very low heat and heat through, gently rotating the pan, for 1–2 minutes; do not allow the soup to boil.

6 Ladle the soup into warm bowls, spoon the spiced melted butter over the top, sprinkle with the mint and serve immediately, accompanied by flatbread.

lamb & rice soup

serves 4
- 150 g/5½ oz lean lamb
- 50 g/1¾ oz rice
- 850 ml/1½ pints lamb stock
- 1 leek, sliced
- 1 garlic clove, thinly sliced
- 2 tsp light soy sauce
- 1 tsp rice wine vinegar
- 1 medium open-cap mushroom, thinly sliced
- salt

1 Using a sharp knife, trim any fat from the lamb and cut the meat into thin strips. Set aside until required.

2 Bring a large pan of lightly salted water to the boil and add the rice. Bring back to the boil, stir once, reduce the heat and cook for 10–15 minutes, until tender. Drain the cooked rice, rinse under cold running water, drain again and set aside.

3 Put the lamb stock in a large saucepan and bring to the boil. Add the lamb strips, leek, garlic, soy sauce and rice wine vinegar, reduce the heat, cover and simmer for 10 minutes, or until the lamb is tender and cooked through.

4 Add the mushroom slices and cooked rice to the saucepan and cook for a further 2–3 minutes, or until the mushroom is completely cooked through.

5 Ladle the soup into warmed bowls and serve immediately.

middle eastern soup with harissa

serves 4

- 2 aubergines
- 3 tbsp olive oil
- 6 lamb shanks
- 1 small onion, chopped
- 400 ml/14 fl oz chicken stock
- 2 litres/3½ pints water
- 400 g/14 oz sweet potato, cut into chunks
- 5-cm/2-inch piece cinnamon stick
- 1 tsp ground cumin
- 2 tbsp chopped fresh coriander

harissa

- 2 red peppers, roasted, peeled, deseeded and chopped
- ½ tsp coriander seeds, dry-fried
- 25 g/1 oz fresh red chillies, chopped
- 2 garlic cloves, chopped
- 2 tsp caraway seeds
- olive oil
- salt

1 Preheat the oven to 200°C/400°F/Gas Mark 6. Prick the aubergines, place on a baking sheet and bake for 1 hour. When cool, peel and chop.

2 Heat the oil in a saucepan. Add the lamb and cook until browned. Add the onion, stock and water. Bring to the boil. Reduce the heat and simmer for 1 hour.

3 For the harissa, process the peppers, coriander seeds, chillies, garlic and caraway seeds in a food processor. With the motor running, add enough oil to make a paste. Add salt to taste, then spoon into a jar. Cover with oil, seal and chill.

4 Remove the shanks from the stock, cut off the meat and chop. Add the sweet potato, cinnamon and cumin to the stock, bring to the boil, cover and simmer for 20 minutes. Discard the cinnamon and process the mixture in a food processor with the aubergine. Return to the saucepan, add the lamb and coriander and heat until hot. Serve with the harissa.

spicy lamb soup with chickpeas & courgettes

serves 4–6

- 1–2 tbsp olive oil
- 450 g/1 lb lean boneless lamb, such as shoulder or neck fillet, trimmed of fat and cut into 1-cm/½-inch cubes
- 1 onion, finely chopped
- 2–3 garlic cloves, crushed
- 1.2 litres/2 pints water
- 400 g/14 oz canned chopped tomatoes
- 1 bay leaf
- ½ tsp dried thyme
- ½ tsp dried oregano
- ⅛ tsp ground cinnamon
- ¼ tsp ground cumin
- ¼ tsp ground turmeric
- 1 tsp harissa, or more to taste
- 400 g/14 oz canned chickpeas, rinsed and drained
- 1 carrot, diced
- 1 potato, diced
- 1 courgette, quartered lengthways and sliced
- 100 g/3½ oz fresh or defrosted frozen green peas
- sprigs of fresh mint or coriander, to garnish

1 Heat 1 tablespoon of the oil in a large saucepan or cast-iron casserole over a medium–high heat. Add the lamb, in batches if necessary to avoid crowding the pan, and cook until evenly browned on all sides, adding a little more oil if needed. Remove the meat with a slotted spoon when browned.

2 Reduce the heat and add the onion and garlic to the pan. Cook, stirring frequently, for 1–2 minutes.

3 Add the water and return all the meat to the pan. Bring just to the boil and skim off any scum that rises to the surface. Reduce the heat and stir in the tomatoes, bay leaf, thyme, oregano, cinnamon, cumin, turmeric and harissa. Simmer for about 1 hour, or until the meat is very tender. Discard the bay leaf.

4 Stir in the chickpeas, carrot and potato and simmer for 15 minutes. Add the courgette and peas and continue simmering for 15–20 minutes, or until all the vegetables are tender.

5 Taste and add more harissa, if desired. Ladle the soup into warmed bowls and garnish with mint or coriander.

asian lamb soup

serves 4

- 150 g/5½ oz lean tender lamb, such as neck fillet or leg steak
- 2 garlic cloves, very finely chopped
- 2 tbsp soy sauce
- 1.2 litres/2 pints chicken stock
- 1 tbsp grated fresh ginger
- 5-cm/2-inch piece lemon grass, sliced into very thin rounds
- ¼ tsp chilli purée, or to taste
- 6–8 cherry tomatoes, quartered
- 4 spring onions, sliced finely
- 50 g/1¾ oz beansprouts, snapped in half
- 2 tbsp fresh coriander leaves
- 1 tsp olive oil

1 Trim all visible fat from the lamb and slice the meat thinly. Cut the slices into bite-sized pieces. Spread the meat in one layer on a plate and sprinkle over the garlic and 1 tablespoon of the soy sauce. Leave to marinate, covered, for at least 10 minutes or up to 1 hour.

2 Put the stock in a saucepan with the ginger, lemon grass, remaining soy sauce and the chilli purée. Bring just to the boil, reduce the heat, cover and simmer for 10–15 minutes.

3 When ready to serve the soup, drop the tomatoes, spring onions, beansprouts and fresh coriander leaves into the simmering stock.

4 Heat the oil in a frying pan and add the lamb with its marinade. Stir-fry the lamb just until it is no longer red and divide among warmed bowls.

5 Ladle over the hot stock and serve immediately.

Mmmm...
poultry

cream of chicken soup

serves 4

- 3 tbsp butter
- 4 shallots, chopped
- 1 leek, sliced
- 450 g/1 lb skinless, boneless chicken breasts, chopped
- 600 ml/1 pint chicken stock
- 1 tbsp chopped fresh parsley
- 1 tbsp chopped fresh thyme, plus extra sprigs to garnish
- 175 ml/6 fl oz double cream
- salt and pepper

1 Melt the butter in a large saucepan over a medium heat. Add the shallots and cook, stirring, for 3 minutes, until slightly softened. Add the leek and cook for a further 5 minutes, stirring. Add the chicken, stock and herbs, and season with salt and pepper. Bring to the boil, then lower the heat and simmer for 25 minutes, until the chicken is tender and cooked through. Remove from the heat and leave to cool for 10 minutes.

2 Transfer the soup to a food processor or blender, in batches if necessary, and process until smooth. Return the soup to the rinsed-out pan and warm over a low heat for 5 minutes.

3 Stir in the cream and cook for a further 2 minutes, then remove from the heat and ladle into serving bowls. Garnish with sprigs of thyme and serve immediately.

chicken & potato soup with bacon

serves 4

- 1 tbsp butter
- 2 garlic cloves, chopped
- 1 onion, sliced
- 250 g/9 oz smoked lean back bacon, chopped
- 2 large leeks, sliced
- 2 tbsp plain flour
- 1 litre/1¾ pints chicken stock
- 800 g/1 lb 12 oz potatoes, chopped
- 200 g/7 oz skinless, boneless chicken breast, chopped
- 4 tbsp double cream
- salt and pepper
- grilled bacon and sprigs of fresh flat-leaf parsley, to garnish

1 Melt the butter in a large saucepan over a medium heat. Add the garlic and onion and cook, stirring, for 3 minutes, until slightly softened. Add the chopped bacon and leeks and cook for a further 3 minutes, stirring.

2 In a bowl, mix the flour with enough stock to make a smooth paste, then stir it into the pan. Cook, stirring, for 2 minutes. Pour in the remaining stock, then add the potatoes and chicken. Season with salt and pepper. Bring to the boil, then lower the heat and simmer for 25 minutes, until the chicken and potatoes are tender and cooked through.

3 Stir in the cream and cook for a further 2 minutes, then remove from the heat and ladle into serving bowls. Garnish with the grilled bacon and flat-leaf parsley, and serve immediately.

chicken & broccoli soup

serves 4–6

- 225 g/8 oz broccoli
- 55 g/2 oz unsalted butter
- 1 onion, chopped
- 25 g/1 oz basmati rice
- 225 g/8 oz skinless, boneless chicken breast, cut into thin strips
- 25 g/1 oz plain wholemeal flour
- 300 ml/10 fl oz milk
- 450 ml/16 fl oz chicken stock
- 55 g/2 oz sweetcorn kernels
- salt and pepper

1 Break the broccoli into small florets and cook in a saucepan of lightly salted boiling water for 3 minutes, drain, then plunge into cold water and reserve.

2 Melt the butter in a saucepan over a medium heat, add the onion, rice and chicken and cook for 5 minutes, stirring frequently.

3 Remove the saucepan from the heat and stir in the flour. Return to the heat and cook for 2 minutes, stirring constantly. Stir in the milk and then the stock. Bring to the boil, stirring constantly, then reduce the heat and simmer for 10 minutes.

4 Drain the broccoli and add to the saucepan with the sweetcorn and salt and pepper to taste. Simmer for 5 minutes, or until the rice is tender, then serve.

chicken, mushroom & barley soup

serves 4

- 75 g/2¾ oz pearl barley, rinsed and drained
- 2 tbsp butter
- 1 large onion, sliced
- 1 large leek, trimmed and sliced
- 1 litre/1¾ pints chicken stock
- 450 g/1 lb skinless, boneless chicken breasts, chopped
- 250 g/9 oz chestnut mushrooms, sliced
- 1 large carrot, peeled and chopped
- 1 tbsp chopped fresh oregano
- 1 bay leaf
- salt and pepper
- sprigs of fresh flat-leaf parsley, to garnish
- fresh crusty bread, to serve

1 Bring a saucepan of water to the boil. Add the barley and boil over a high heat for 5 minutes, skimming the surface when necessary. Remove from the heat and reserve.

2 Melt the butter in a large saucepan. Add the onion and cook over a medium heat, stirring, for 3 minutes, until slightly softened. Add the leek and cook for a further 4 minutes, stirring. Stir in the stock, then drain the barley and add to the pan. Season with salt and pepper. Bring to the boil, then lower the heat and simmer for 45 minutes. Add the chicken, mushrooms, carrot, oregano and bay leaf. Cook for a further 30 minutes.

3 Remove from the heat and discard the bay leaf. Ladle into serving bowls, garnish with sprigs of fresh flat-leaf parsley and serve with fresh crusty bread.

chicken gumbo soup

serves 6
- 2 tbsp olive oil
- 4 tbsp plain flour
- 1 onion, finely chopped
- 1 small green pepper, deseeded and finely chopped
- 1 celery stick, finely chopped
- 1.2 litres/2 pints chicken stock
- 400 g/14 oz canned chopped tomatoes
- 3 garlic cloves, finely chopped or crushed
- 125 g/4½ oz okra, stems removed, cut into 5 mm/¼ inch thick slices
- 50 g/1¾ oz white rice
- 200 g/7 oz cooked chicken, cubed
- 115 g/4 oz cooked garlic sausage, sliced or cubed
- salt and pepper

1 Heat the oil in a large heavy-based saucepan over a medium–low heat and stir in the flour. Cook for about 15 minutes, stirring occasionally, until the mixture is a rich golden brown.

2 Add the onion, green pepper and celery and continue cooking for about 10 minutes until the onion softens.

3 Slowly pour in the stock and bring to the boil, stirring well and scraping the bottom of the pan to mix in the flour. Remove the pan from the heat.

4 Add the tomatoes and garlic. Stir in the okra and rice and season to taste with salt and pepper. Reduce the heat, cover and simmer for 20 minutes, or until the okra is tender.

5 Add the chicken and sausage and continue simmering for about 10 minutes. Taste and adjust the seasoning, if necessary, and ladle into warmed bowls to serve.

mulligatawny soup

serves 4–6

- 55 g/2 oz butter
- 2 onions, chopped
- 1 small turnip, cut into small dice
- 2 carrots, finely sliced
- 1 eating apple, cored, peeled and chopped
- 2 tbsp mild curry powder
- 1.2 litres/2 pints chicken stock
- juice of ½ lemon
- 175 g/6 oz cold cooked chicken, cut into small pieces
- 2 tbsp chopped fresh coriander, plus extra to garnish
- salt and pepper
- 55 g/2 oz cooked rice, to serve

1 Melt the butter in a large saucepan over a medium heat, add the onions and sauté gently until soft but not brown.

2 Add the turnip, carrots and apple and continue to cook for a further 3–4 minutes.

3 Stir in the curry powder until the vegetables are well coated, then pour in the stock. Bring to the boil, cover and simmer for about 45 minutes. Season well with salt and pepper to taste and add the lemon juice.

4 Transfer the soup to a food processor or blender. Process until smooth and return to the rinsed-out saucepan. Add the chicken and coriander to the saucepan and heat through.

5 Place a spoonful of rice in each serving bowl and pour the soup over the top. Garnish with coriander and serve.

cock-a-leekie

serves 4–6

- 25 g/1 oz butter
- 350 g/12 oz boneless chicken, diced
- 350 g/12 oz leeks, cut into 2.5-cm/1-inch pieces
- 1.2 litres/2 pints chicken stock
- 1 bouquet garni (see page 86)
- 8 pitted prunes, halved
- 70 g/2½ oz cooked rice
- 1 red pepper, diced (optional)
- salt and white pepper

1 Melt the butter in a large saucepan. Add the chicken and leeks and cook for 8 minutes.

2 Add the chicken stock and bouquet garni to the saucepan and stir well, then season with salt and pepper to taste. Bring to the boil and simmer for 45 minutes.

3 Add the prunes to the saucepan with the cooked rice and diced pepper, if using, and simmer for about 20 minutes.

4 Remove the bouquet garni from the soup and discard. Ladle into warmed soup bowls and serve immediately.

chicken &
sweetcorn soup

serves 6

- 1 roasted chicken, about 1.3 kg/3 lb
- ½ tsp saffron threads
- 3 tbsp corn oil
- 2 onions, thinly sliced
- 3 celery sticks, sliced
- 1.7 litres/3 pints vegetable stock
- 8 black peppercorns
- 1 mace blade
- 115 g/4 oz egg noodles
- 400 g/14 oz frozen sweetcorn
- pinch of dried sage
- 2 tbsp chopped fresh parsley
- salt and pepper

1 Remove the skin from the chicken, cut the meat off the bones and cut into small pieces. Put the saffron into a bowl, pour in hot water to cover and leave to soak.

2 Heat the oil in a saucepan. Add the onions and celery and cook over a low heat, stirring occasionally, for 5 minutes, until softened. Increase the heat to medium, pour in the stock, add the peppercorns and mace and bring to the boil. Reduce the heat and simmer for 25 minutes.

3 Increase the heat to medium, add the chicken, noodles, sweetcorn, sage, parsley and saffron with its soaking water, season to taste with salt and pepper and bring back to the boil. Reduce the heat and simmer for a further 20 minutes.

4 Remove the pan from the heat, taste and adjust the seasoning, if necessary, ladle into warmed bowls and serve immediately.

chicken & almond soup

serves 6
- 115 g/4 oz butter
- 2 leeks, chopped
- 2-cm/¾-inch piece of fresh ginger, finely chopped
- 175 g/6 oz skinless, boneless chicken, diced
- 2 carrots, chopped
- 85 g/3 oz shelled fresh or frozen peas
- 2 green chillies, deseeded and chopped
- 140 g/5 oz ground almonds
- 1 tbsp chopped fresh coriander, plus extra to garnish
- 700 ml/1¼ pints basic vegetable stock
- 350 ml/12 fl oz single cream
- salt and pepper
- grated Parmesan cheese, to serve

1 Melt the butter in a saucepan. Add the leeks and ginger and cook over a low heat, stirring occasionally, for 5 minutes, until softened. Add the chicken, carrots, peas, chillies and ground almonds and cook, stirring constantly, for 10 minutes.

2 Stir in the coriander, remove from the heat and leave to cool slightly. Spoon the chicken mixture into a food processor or blender and process until very finely chopped. Add the stock and process to a purée.

3 Return the mixture to the pan, season to taste with salt and pepper and bring to the boil. Reduce the heat to very low and gradually stir in the cream; do not let the soup come back to the boil. Simmer, stirring frequently, for 2 minutes. Ladle into warmed bowls, sprinkle with chopped coriander and Parmesan and serve.

whole chicken soup

serves 6–8

- 100 g/3½ oz Yunnan ham or ordinary ham, chopped
- 2 dried Chinese mushrooms, soaked in warm water for 20 minutes
- 85 g/3 oz fresh or canned bamboo shoots, rinsed (if using fresh shoots, boil in water first for 30 minutes)
- 1 whole chicken
- 1 tbsp slivered spring onion
- 8 slices fresh ginger
- 225 g/8 oz lean pork, chopped
- 2 tsp Shaoxing rice wine
- 3 litres/5¼ pints water
- 2 tsp salt
- 300 g/10½ oz Chinese cabbage, cut into large chunks

sesame & spring onion dipping sauce

- 2 tbsp light soy sauce
- ¼ tsp sesame oil
- 2 tsp finely chopped spring onion

1 To make the dipping sauce, combine the ingredients and set aside.

2 Blanch the Yunnan ham in a large saucepan of boiling water for 30 seconds. Skim the surface, then remove the ham and set aside. Squeeze out any excess water from the mushrooms, then finely slice and discard any tough stems. Chop the bamboo shoots into small cubes.

3 Stuff the chicken with the spring onion and ginger. Put all the ingredients except the cabbage and dipping sauce in a casserole. Bring to the boil, then lower the heat and simmer, covered, for 1 hour. Add the cabbage and simmer for a further 3 minutes.

4 Remove the chicken skin before serving, then tear the meat and place in individual bowls. Add pieces of vegetable and the other meats and pour the soup on top. Serve the soup with the sesame and spring onion sauce for dipping the chicken pieces into.

143

chicken & lentil soup

serves 6

- 3 tbsp olive oil
- 1 large onion, chopped
- 2 leeks, chopped
- 2 carrots, chopped
- 2 celery sticks, chopped
- 175 g/6 oz button mushrooms, chopped
- 4 tbsp dry white wine
- 1.2 litres/2 pints vegetable stock
- 1 bay leaf
- 2 tsp dried mixed herbs
- 175 g/6 oz Puy lentils
- 350 g/12 oz boneless cooked chicken, diced
- salt and pepper

1 Heat the oil in a large saucepan. Add the onion, leeks, carrots, celery and mushrooms and cook over a low heat, stirring occasionally, for 5–7 minutes, until softened but not coloured.

2 Increase the heat to medium, pour in the wine and cook for 2–3 minutes, until the alcohol has evaporated, then pour in the stock. Bring to the boil, add the bay leaf and herbs, reduce the heat, cover and simmer for 30 minutes.

3 Add the lentils, re-cover the pan and simmer, stirring occasionally, for a further 40 minutes, until they are tender.

4 Stir in the chicken, season to taste with salt and pepper and simmer for a further 5–10 minutes, until heated through. Remove and discard the bay leaf and serve immediately.

italian chicken soup

serves 4
- 450 g/1 lb skinless, boneless chicken breast, cut into thin strips
- 1.2 litres/2 pints chicken stock
- 150 ml/5 fl oz double cream
- 115 g/4 oz dried vermicelli
- 1 tbsp cornflour
- 3 tbsp milk
- 175 g/6 oz canned sweetcorn kernels, drained
- salt and pepper

1 Place the chicken in a large saucepan and pour in the chicken stock and cream. Bring to the boil, then reduce the heat and simmer for 20 minutes.

2 Meanwhile, bring a large, heavy-based saucepan of lightly salted water to the boil. Add the pasta, return to the boil and cook for 4–5 minutes, or until just tender but still firm to the bite. Drain the pasta well and keep warm.

3 Season the soup to taste with salt and pepper. Mix the cornflour and milk together until a smooth paste forms, then stir it into the soup. Add the sweetcorn and pasta and heat through. Ladle the soup into warmed soup bowls and serve immediately.

chicken & rice soup

serves 4

- 1.5 litres/2¾ pints chicken stock
- 2 small carrots, very thinly sliced
- 1 celery stick, finely diced
- 1 baby leek, halved lengthways and thinly sliced
- 115 g/4 oz petit pois, defrosted if frozen
- 175 g/6 oz cooked rice
- 150 g/5½ oz cooked chicken, sliced
- 2 tsp chopped fresh tarragon
- 1 tbsp chopped fresh parsley
- salt and pepper
- sprigs of fresh parsley, to garnish

1 Put the stock in a large saucepan and add the carrots, celery and leek. Bring to the boil, reduce the heat to low and simmer gently, partially covered, for 10 minutes.

2 Stir in the petit pois, rice and chicken and continue cooking for a further 10–15 minutes, or until the vegetables are tender.

3 Add the chopped tarragon and parsley, then taste and adjust the seasoning, adding salt and pepper as needed.

4 Ladle the soup into warmed bowls, garnish with parsley and serve.

chicken soup with leeks & rice

serves 6

- 2 tbsp olive oil
- 3 leeks, chopped
- 6 skinless, boneless chicken thighs, diced
- 55 g/2 oz long-grain rice
- 1.3 litres/2¼ pints vegetable stock
- dash of Worcestershire sauce
- 6 fresh chives, chopped
- 6 thin bacon rashers
- 2 tbsp chopped fresh parsley
- salt and pepper

1 Heat the oil in a saucepan. Add the leeks and cook over a low heat, stirring occasionally, for 5 minutes, until softened. Add the chicken, increase the heat to medium and cook, stirring frequently, for 2 minutes. Add the rice and cook, stirring constantly, for 2 minutes more.

2 Pour in the stock, add the Worcestershire sauce and chives and bring to the boil. Reduce the heat, cover and simmer for 20–25 minutes.

3 Meanwhile, preheat the grill. Grill the bacon for 2–4 minutes on each side, until crisp. Remove and leave to cool, then crumble.

4 Season the soup to taste with salt and pepper and stir in the parsley. Ladle into warmed bowls, sprinkle with the crumbled bacon and serve.

thai chicken soup

serves 4

- 1 tbsp sesame oil or chilli oil
- 2 garlic cloves, chopped
- 2 spring onions, trimmed and sliced
- 1 leek, trimmed and finely sliced
- 1 tbsp grated fresh ginger
- 1 fresh red chilli, deseeded and finely chopped
- 350 g/12 oz skinless, boneless chicken breasts, cut into strips
- 850 ml/1½ pints chicken stock
- 2 tbsp rice wine
- 1 tbsp chopped lemon grass
- 6 kaffir lime leaves, finely shredded
- 200 g/7 oz fine egg noodles
- salt and pepper

1 Heat the oil in a wok or large saucepan. Add the garlic and cook over a medium heat, stirring, for 1 minute, then add the spring onions, leek, ginger and chilli and cook, stirring, for a further 3 minutes. Add the chicken, stock and rice wine, bring to the boil and simmer for 20 minutes. Stir in the lemon grass and kaffir lime leaves.

2 Bring a separate saucepan of water to the boil and add the noodles. Cook for 3 minutes, drain well, then add them to the soup. Season to taste with salt and pepper. Cook for a further 2 minutes. Remove from the heat, ladle into individual bowls and serve hot.

chicken noodle soup

serves 4–6

- 2 skinless chicken breasts
- 1.2 litres/2 pints water or chicken stock
- 3 carrots, peeled and sliced into 5-mm/1/4-inch slices
- 85 g/3 oz vermicelli (or other small noodles)
- salt and pepper
- fresh tarragon leaves, to garnish

1 Place the chicken breasts in a large saucepan, add the water and bring to a simmer. Cook for 25–30 minutes. Skim any scum from the surface if necessary. Remove the chicken from the stock and keep warm.

2 While the stock is simmering, add the carrots and vermicelli and cook for 4–5 minutes.

3 Thinly slice or shred the chicken breasts and place in warmed serving dishes.

4 Season the soup to taste with salt and pepper and pour over the chicken. Serve immediately garnished with the tarragon.

thai chicken-coconut soup

serves 4

- 115 g/4 oz dried cellophane noodles
- 1.2 litres/2 pints chicken or vegetable stock
- 1 lemon grass stalk, crushed
- 1-cm/½-inch piece fresh ginger, very finely chopped
- 2 fresh kaffir lime leaves, thinly sliced
- 1 fresh red chilli, or to taste, deseeded and thinly sliced
- 2 skinless, boneless chicken breasts, thinly sliced
- 200 ml/7 fl oz coconut cream
- 2 tbsp nam pla (fish sauce)
- 1 tbsp fresh lime juice
- 55 g/2 oz beansprouts
- 4 spring onions, green part only, finely sliced
- fresh coriander leaves, to garnish

1 Soak the dried noodles in a large bowl with enough lukewarm water to cover for 20 minutes, until soft. Alternatively, cook according to the packet instructions. Drain well and set aside.

2 Meanwhile, bring the stock to the boil in a large saucepan over a high heat. Lower the heat, add the lemon grass, ginger, lime leaves and chilli and simmer for 5 minutes. Add the chicken and continue simmering for a further 3 minutes, or until cooked. Stir in the coconut cream, nam pla and lime juice and continue simmering for 3 minutes. Add the beansprouts and spring onions and simmer for a further 1 minute. Taste and gradually add extra nam pla or lime juice at this point, if needed. Remove and discard the lemon grass stalk.

3 Divide the vermicelli noodles between 4 bowls. Bring the soup back to the boil, then add the soup to each bowl. The heat of the soup will warm the noodles. Garnish with coriander leaves and serve immediately.

oriental chicken balls & greens in broth

serves 6

- 2 litres/3½ pints chicken stock
- 85 g/3 oz shiitake mushrooms, thinly sliced
- 175 g/6 oz pak choi or other Oriental greens, sliced into thin ribbons
- 6 spring onions, finely sliced
- salt and pepper

chicken balls

- 25 g/1 oz chicken, minced
- 25 g/1 oz fresh spinach leaves, finely chopped
- 2 spring onions, finely chopped
- 1 garlic clove, very finely chopped
- pinch of Oriental 5-spice powder
- 1 tsp soy sauce

1 To make the chicken balls, put the chicken, spinach, spring onions and garlic in a bowl. Add the 5-spice powder and soy sauce and mix until combined.

2 Shape the chicken mixture into 24 balls. Place them in one layer in a steamer that will fit over the top of a saucepan.

3 Bring the stock just to the boil in a saucepan that will accommodate the steamer. Regulate the heat so that the liquid bubbles gently. Add the mushrooms to the stock and place the steamer, covered, on top of the pan. Steam for 10 minutes. Remove the steamer and set aside on a plate.

4 Add the pak choi and spring onions to the pan and cook gently in the stock for 3–4 minutes, or until the leaves are wilted. Taste the soup and adjust the seasoning, if necessary.

5 Divide the chicken balls evenly between warmed bowls and ladle the soup over them. Serve immediately.

chicken soup with ginger & coconut milk

serves 4

- 400 g/14 oz skinless, boneless chicken breasts, cut into strips
- 100 g/3½ oz Thai fragrant rice
- 1 lemon grass stalk, bruised
- 4 garlic cloves, roughly chopped
- 2 green chillies, deseeded and sliced
- 4 kaffir lime leaves, torn
- 2.5-cm/1-inch piece fresh ginger, chopped
- 4 tbsp chopped fresh coriander, plus extra to garnish
- 1.5 litres/2¾ pints basic vegetable stock
- 400 ml/14 fl oz canned coconut milk
- 4 spring onions, thinly sliced
- 115 g/4 oz baby corn cobs
- 115 g/4 oz button mushrooms, halved
- salt
- chopped red chilli, to garnish

1 Put the chicken, rice, lemon grass, garlic, chillies, lime leaves, ginger and coriander into a saucepan, pour in the stock and coconut milk and bring to the boil over a medium heat, stirring occasionally. Reduce the heat, cover and simmer for 1 hour.

2 Remove the pan from the heat and leave to cool slightly. Remove and discard the lemon grass and kaffir lime leaves. Ladle the soup into a food processor or blender, in batches if necessary, and process to a purée.

3 Return the soup to the rinsed-out pan, season to taste with salt and add the spring onions, corn cobs and mushrooms. Bring back to the boil, then reduce the heat and simmer for 5 minutes.

4 Remove the pan from the heat. Ladle the soup into warmed bowls, garnish with chopped coriander and chilli and serve immediately.

turkey soup with rice, mushrooms & sage

serves 4–5

- 3 tbsp butter
- 1 onion, finely chopped
- 1 celery stick, finely chopped
- 25 large fresh sage leaves, finely chopped
- 4 tbsp plain flour
- 1.2 litres/2 pints turkey or chicken stock
- 100 g/3½ oz brown rice
- 250 g/9 oz mushrooms, sliced
- 200 g/7 oz cooked turkey, diced
- 200 ml/7 fl oz double cream
- salt and pepper
- sprigs of fresh sage, to garnish
- freshly grated Parmesan cheese, to serve

1 Melt half the butter in a large saucepan over a medium–low heat. Add the onion, celery and sage and cook for 3–4 minutes, until the onion is softened, stirring frequently. Stir in the flour and continue cooking for 2 minutes.

2 Slowly add about one quarter of the stock and stir well. Pour in the remaining stock, stirring to combine completely, and bring just to the boil.

3 Stir in the rice and season with salt and pepper. Reduce the heat and simmer gently, partially covered, for about 30 minutes, until the rice is just tender, stirring occasionally.

4 Meanwhile, melt the remaining butter in a large frying pan over a medium heat. Add the mushrooms and season with salt and pepper. Cook for about 8 minutes, until they are golden brown.

5 Add the turkey and mushrooms to the soup and stir in the cream. Continue simmering for about 10 minutes, until heated through. Ladle into warmed bowls, garnish with sage and serve with Parmesan cheese.

lemon turkey soup with mushrooms

serves 4

- 350 g/12 oz boneless turkey, cut into 1-cm/½-inch pieces
- 1 litre/1¾ pints chicken stock
- 1 onion, quartered
- 2 carrots, thinly sliced
- 2 garlic cloves, halved
- 1 pared strip lemon rind
- 1 bay leaf
- 1 tbsp butter
- 350 g/12 oz small button mushrooms, quartered
- 4 tbsp cornflour
- 125 ml/4 fl oz double cream
- freshly grated nutmeg
- fresh lemon juice, to taste (optional)
- 1–2 tbsp chopped fresh flat-leaf parsley
- salt and pepper

1 Put the turkey in a large saucepan and add the stock. Bring just to the boil. Add the onion, carrots, garlic, lemon rind and bay leaf. Season with salt and pepper. Reduce the heat and simmer, partially covered, for about 45 minutes, stirring occasionally, until the turkey is cooked.

2 Remove the turkey and carrots with a slotted spoon and reserve, covered. Strain the stock into a clean saucepan. Discard the onion and garlic, lemon rind and bay leaf.

3 Melt the butter in a frying pan over a medium–high heat. Add the mushrooms, season, and fry gently until lightly golden. Reserve with the turkey and carrots.

4 Mix together the cornflour and cream. Bring the stock just to the boil and whisk in the cream mixture. Boil gently for 2–3 minutes until it thickens, whisking constantly.

5 Add the reserved meat and vegetables to the soup and simmer over a low heat for about 5 minutes until heated through. Add the nutmeg and a squeeze of lemon juice, if using. Stir in the parsley, then ladle into warmed bowls and serve.

turkey, leek & stilton soup

serves 4
- 4 tbsp butter
- 1 large onion, chopped
- 1 leek, trimmed and sliced
- 325 g/11½ oz cooked turkey meat, sliced
- 600 ml/1 pint chicken stock
- 150 g/5½ oz Stilton cheese, crumbled
- 150 ml/5 fl oz double cream
- 1 tbsp chopped fresh tarragon
- pepper
- fresh tarragon leaves and croûtons (see page 9), to garnish

1 Melt the butter in a saucepan over a medium heat. Add the onion and cook, stirring, for 4 minutes, until slightly softened. Add the leek and cook for another 3 minutes.

2 Add the turkey to the pan and pour in the stock. Bring to the boil, then reduce the heat and simmer gently, stirring occasionally, for about 15 minutes. Remove from the heat and leave to cool a little.

3 Transfer half of the soup into a food processor and blend until smooth. Return the mixture to the pan with the rest of the soup, stir in the Stilton, cream and tarragon and season with pepper. Reheat gently, stirring. Remove from the heat, ladle into warmed soup bowls, garnish with tarragon and croûtons and serve.

turkey & lentil soup

serves 4

- 1 tbsp olive oil
- 1 garlic clove, chopped
- 1 large onion, chopped
- 200 g/7 oz mushrooms, sliced
- 1 red pepper, deseeded and chopped
- 6 tomatoes, peeled, deseeded and chopped
- 1.2 litres/2 pints chicken stock
- 150 ml/5 fl oz red wine
- 85 g/3 oz cauliflower florets
- 1 carrot, chopped
- 200 g/7 oz red lentils
- 350 g/12 oz cooked turkey, chopped
- 1 courgette, chopped
- 1 tbsp shredded fresh basil
- salt and pepper
- sprigs of fresh basil, to garnish

1 Heat the oil in a large saucepan. Add the garlic and onion and cook over a medium heat, stirring, for 3 minutes, until slightly softened. Add the mushrooms, red pepper and tomatoes and cook for a further 5 minutes, stirring. Pour in the stock and red wine, then add the cauliflower, carrot and red lentils. Season to taste with salt and pepper. Bring to the boil, then lower the heat and simmer the soup gently for 25 minutes, until the vegetables are tender and cooked through.

2 Add the turkey and courgette to the pan and cook for 10 minutes. Stir in the shredded basil and cook for a further 5 minutes, then remove from the heat and ladle into serving bowls. Garnish with basil and serve immediately.

oriental duck broth

serves 4-6

- 2 duck leg quarters, skinned
- 1 litre/1¾ pints water
- 600 ml/1 pint chicken stock
- 2.5-cm/1-inch piece fresh ginger, sliced
- 1 large carrot, sliced
- 1 onion, sliced
- 1 leek, sliced
- 3 garlic cloves, crushed
- 1 tsp black peppercorns
- 2 tbsp soy sauce, or to taste
- 1 small carrot, cut into thin strips or slivers
- 1 small leek, cut into thin strips or slivers
- 100 g/3½ oz shiitake mushrooms, thinly sliced
- 25 g/1 oz watercress leaves
- salt and pepper

1 Put the duck in a large saucepan with the water. Bring just to the boil and skim off the scum that rises to the surface. Add the stock, ginger, carrot, onion, leek, garlic, peppercorns and soy sauce. Reduce the heat and simmer, partially covered, for 1½ hours.

2 Remove the duck from the stock and set aside. When the duck is cool enough to handle, remove the meat from the bones and slice thinly or shred into bite-sized pieces, discarding any fat.

3 Strain the stock and press the vegetables with the back of a spoon to extract all the liquid. Remove as much fat as possible. Discard the vegetables and herbs.

4 Bring the stock just to the boil in a clean saucepan and add the strips of carrot and leek, the mushrooms and duck meat. Reduce the heat and cook gently for 5 minutes, or until the carrot is just tender.

5 Stir in the watercress and continue simmering for 1–2 minutes until it is wilted. Taste the soup and adjust the seasoning if needed, adding a little more soy sauce, if wished. Ladle the soup into warmed bowls and serve immediately.

duck with spring onion soup

serves 4

- 2 duck breasts, skin on
- 2 tbsp red curry paste
- 2 tbsp vegetable or groundnut oil
- bunch of spring onions, chopped, plus extra to garnish
- 2 garlic cloves, crushed
- 5-cm/2-inch piece fresh ginger, grated
- 2 carrots, thinly sliced
- 1 red pepper, deseeded and cut into strips
- 1 litre/1¾ pints chicken stock
- 2 tbsp sweet chilli sauce
- 3–4 tbsp Thai soy sauce
- 400 g/14 oz canned straw mushrooms, drained

1 Slash the skin of the duck 3 or 4 times with a sharp knife and rub in the curry paste. Cook the duck breasts, skin-side down, in a wok or frying pan over a high heat for 2–3 minutes. Turn over, reduce the heat and cook for a further 3–4 minutes, until cooked through. Lift out and slice thickly. Set aside and keep warm.

2 Meanwhile, heat the oil in a wok or large frying pan and stir-fry half the spring onions, the garlic, ginger, carrots and red pepper for 2–3 minutes. Pour in the stock and add the chilli sauce, soy sauce and mushrooms. Bring to the boil, lower the heat and simmer for 4–5 minutes.

3 Ladle the soup into warmed bowls, top with the duck slices and garnish with the remaining spring onions. Serve immediately.

Mmmm...
fish & seafood

fisherman's soup

serves 6

- 900 g/2 lb fillets of mixed white fish and shellfish, such as cod, flounder, halibut, monkfish, sea bass, whiting and peeled prawns
- 150 ml/5 fl oz olive oil
- 2 large onions, sliced
- 2 celery sticks, thinly sliced
- 2 garlic cloves, chopped
- 150 ml/5 fl oz white wine
- 4 canned tomatoes, chopped
- pared rind of 1 orange
- 1 tsp chopped fresh thyme
- 2 tbsp chopped fresh parsley
- 2 bay leaves
- salt and pepper
- croûtons (see page 9) and sprigs of fresh thyme, to garnish
- lemon wedges, to serve

1 Cut the fish into fairly large, thick serving portions, discarding any skin.

2 Heat the oil in a large saucepan, add the onions, celery and garlic and fry for 5 minutes, until soft.

3 Add the fish and prawns to the pan then add the wine, tomatoes, orange rind, thyme, parsley, bay leaves, salt and pepper and enough cold water to cover. Bring to the boil, then simmer, uncovered, for 15 minutes.

4 Garnish the soup with croûtons and thyme, and serve hot, with lemon wedges.

fish & sweet potato soup

serves 6

- 350 g/12 oz white fish fillet, skinned
- 250 g/9 oz sweet potato, diced
- 1 onion, chopped
- 2 carrots, diced
- ½ tsp ground cinnamon
- 1.7 litres/3 pints vegetable stock
- 400 g/14 oz live clams
- 150 ml/5 fl oz dry white wine
- 225 ml/8 fl oz single cream
- salt and pepper
- extra virgin olive oil, for drizzling
- chopped fresh parsley, to garnish

1 Put the fish, sweet potato, onion, carrots and cinnamon into a saucepan, pour in 1 litre/1¾ pints of the stock and bring to the boil. Reduce the heat, cover and simmer for 30 minutes.

2 Meanwhile, scrub the clams under cold running water and remove any with broken shells or that do not shut immediately when sharply tapped. Put them into a saucepan, pour in the wine, cover and cook over a high heat, shaking the pan occasionally, for 3–5 minutes, until the clams have opened. Remove from the heat and lift out the clams with a slotted spoon, reserving the cooking liquid. Discard any clams that remain shut and remove the remainder from the half shells. Strain the cooking liquid through a fine strainer into a bowl.

3 Remove the pan of fish and vegetables from the heat and leave to cool slightly, then ladle the mixture into a food processor or blender, and process until smooth.

4 Return to the pan, add the remaining stock and reserved cooking liquid and bring back to the boil. Reduce the heat and gradually stir in the cream; do not allow the soup to boil. Add the clams, season to taste with salt and pepper and simmer, stirring frequently, for 2 minutes. Drizzle with olive oil, garnish with parsley and serve.

breton fish soup with cider & sorrel

serves 4

- 2 tsp butter
- 1 large leek, thinly sliced
- 2 shallots, finely chopped
- 125 ml/4 fl oz dry cider
- 300 ml/10 fl oz fish stock
- 250 g/9 oz potatoes, diced
- 1 bay leaf
- 4 tbsp plain flour
- 200 ml/7 fl oz milk
- 200 ml/7 fl oz double cream
- 55 g/2 oz fresh sorrel leaves, finely chopped
- 350 g/12 oz skinless monkfish or cod fillet, cut into 2.5-cm/1-inch pieces
- salt

1 Melt the butter in a large saucepan over a medium–low heat. Add the leek and shallots and cook for about 5 minutes, stirring frequently, until they start to soften. Add the cider and bring to the boil.

2 Stir in the stock, potatoes and bay leaf with a large pinch of salt (unless the stock is salty) and bring back to the boil. Reduce the heat, cover and cook gently for 10 minutes.

3 Put the flour in a small bowl and very slowly whisk in a few tablespoons of the milk to make a thick paste. Stir in a little more to make a smooth liquid.

4 Adjust the heat so the soup bubbles gently. Stir in the flour mixture and cook, stirring frequently, for 5 minutes. Add the remaining milk and half the cream. Continue cooking for about 10 minutes, until the potatoes are tender.

5 Add the sorrel and combine with the remaining cream. Stir the sorrel cream into the soup and add the fish. Continue cooking, stirring occasionally, for about 3 minutes, until the monkfish stiffens or the cod just begins to flake. Remove and discard the bay leaf and ladle into bowls and serve.

mixed fish soup

serves 4

- 1 tbsp butter
- 2 shallots, chopped
- 1 leek, trimmed and sliced
- 3 tbsp plain flour
- 500 ml/18 fl oz fish stock
- 1 bay leaf
- 500 ml/18 fl oz milk
- 2 tbsp dry sherry
- 2 tbsp lemon juice
- 300 g/10½ oz haddock fillets, skinned
- 300 g/10½ oz cod fillets, skinned
- 200 g/7 oz canned or freshly cooked crabmeat
- 150 g/5½ oz canned sweetcorn, drained
- 200 ml/7 fl oz double cream
- salt and pepper
- sprigs of fresh dill and wedges of lemon, to garnish

1 Melt the butter in a large saucepan over a medium heat. Add the shallots and leek and cook, stirring, for about 3 minutes, until slightly softened. In a bowl, mix the flour with enough stock to make a smooth paste, then stir it into the pan. Cook, stirring, for 2 minutes, then gradually stir in the remaining stock. Add the bay leaf and season with salt and pepper. Bring to the boil, then lower the heat. Pour in the milk and sherry, and stir in the lemon juice. Simmer for 15 minutes.

2 Rinse the haddock and cod fillets under cold running water, then drain and cut into bite-sized chunks. Add to the soup with the crabmeat and sweetcorn. Cook for 15 minutes, until the fish is tender and cooked through. Stir in the cream. Cook for another 2–3 minutes, then remove from the heat and discard the bay leaf.

3 Ladle into serving bowls, garnish with sprigs of fresh dill and lemon wedges and serve.

miso fish soup

serves 4

- 850 ml/1½ pints fish stock or vegetable stock
- 2.5-cm/1-inch piece fresh ginger, grated
- 1 tbsp mirin or dry sherry
- 1 fresh bird's eye chilli, deseeded and finely sliced
- 1 carrot, about 85 g/3 oz, peeled and thinly sliced
- 55 g/2 oz daikon, peeled and cut into thin strips or ½ bunch radishes, trimmed and sliced
- 1 yellow pepper, deseeded and cut into thin strips
- 85 g/3 oz shiitake mushrooms, sliced if large
- 40 g/1½ oz thread egg noodles
- 225 g/8 oz sole fillets, skinned and cut into strips
- 1 tbsp miso paste
- 4 spring onions, trimmed and shredded

1 Pour the stock into a large saucepan and add the ginger, mirin and chilli. Bring to the boil then reduce the heat and simmer for 5 minutes.

2 Add the carrot with the daikon, pepper strips, mushrooms and noodles and simmer for a further 3 minutes.

3 Add the fish strips with the miso paste and continue to cook for 2 minutes, or until the fish is tender. Divide equally between 4 serving bowls, top with the spring onions and serve immediately.

fish soup with semolina & dill dumplings

serves 6
- 85 g/3 oz chorizo, diced
- 500 g/1 lb 2 oz white fish fillets, such as cod or monkfish skinned and diced
- 1 tbsp sweet paprika
- pinch of cayenne pepper
- 1.4 litres/2½ pints vegetable stock
- 4 potatoes, diced
- 4 tomatoes, peeled and diced
- 1 tbsp chopped fresh parsley
- salt and pepper

semolina & dill dumplings
- 85 g/3 oz fine semolina
- pinch of salt
- 1 tbsp chopped fresh dill
- 1 egg
- 3 tbsp milk

1 Put the chorizo into a heavy-based saucepan and cook over a medium–low heat, stirring frequently, for 5 minutes until lightly browned. Add the fish and cook, occasionally stirring gently, for 2 minutes.

2 Sprinkle in the paprika and cayenne pepper, pour in the stock and bring to the boil. Reduce the heat, cover and simmer for 10 minutes.

3 Add the potatoes, tomatoes and parsley, stir gently, re-cover the pan and simmer for 10 minutes.

4 Meanwhile, make the semolina and dill dumplings. Mix together the semolina, salt and dill in a bowl. Lightly beat together the egg and milk in another bowl, then stir into the dry ingredients until thoroughly combined. Cover and leave to rest in the refrigerator for 10 minutes.

5 Scoop up tablespoonfuls of the dumpling mixture and add them to the soup. Re-cover the pan and simmer for a further 10 minutes. Season to taste with salt and pepper and serve immediately.

genoese fish soup

serves 4

- 25 g/1 oz butter
- 1 onion, chopped
- 1 garlic clove, finely chopped
- 55 g/2 oz rindless streaky bacon, diced
- 2 celery sticks, chopped
- 400 g/14 oz canned chopped tomatoes
- 150 ml/5 fl oz dry white wine
- 300 ml/10 fl oz fish stock
- 4 fresh basil leaves, torn
- 1 tbsp chopped fresh flat-leaf parsley, plus extra to garnish
- 450 g/1 lb white fish fillets, such as cod or monkfish, skinned and cut into bite-sized pieces
- 115 g/4 oz cooked peeled prawns
- salt and pepper

1 Melt the butter in a large, heavy-based saucepan. Add the onion and garlic and cook over a low heat, stirring occasionally, for 5 minutes, or until softened.

2 Add the streaky bacon and celery and cook, stirring frequently, for a further 2 minutes.

3 Add the tomatoes, wine, stock, basil and the parsley. Season to taste with salt and pepper. Bring to the boil, then reduce the heat and simmer for 10 minutes.

4 Add the fish and cook for 5 minutes, or until it is opaque. Add the prawns and heat through gently for 3 minutes. Ladle into warmed serving bowls, garnish with the chopped parsley and serve immediately.

spicy & sour fish soup

serves 6

- 450 g/1 lb skinless, boneless cod fillets, cut into large chunks
- 100 ml/3½ fl oz tamarind concentrate
- 225 g/8 oz peeled and cored ripe pineapple, cut into bite-sized chunks
- 1 large ripe tomato, peeled, halved, deseeded and cut into 8 wedges
- 2 or more red bird's eye chillies, deseeded and thinly sliced into rounds
- 1 tbsp nam pla (fish sauce)
- 12 fresh Thai basil leaves, freshly torn
- 6 fresh saw leaves, freshly torn, or 5 g/1/8 oz fresh coriander leaves
- salt and pepper
- garlic oil, to garnish

light fish stock

- 2.8 litres/5 pints water
- 1.1 kg/2½ lb fish heads and bones
- 25 g/1 oz fresh ginger, peeled and thinly sliced
- 4 spring onions, trimmed and crushed
- 2–3 tbsp nam pla (fish sauce)

1 For the stock, put the water, fish heads and bones in a large saucepan and bring to the boil over a high heat. Reduce the heat to medium-low, then add the ginger, spring onions and nam pla and simmer for 1½ hours, or until reduced by about half, skimming off any foam. Strain the stock, discarding the solids, and remove any fat.

2 Season the fish to taste with salt and pepper. Cover with clingfilm and refrigerate for up to 30 minutes.

3 Pour the stock into a medium saucepan and bring to a gentle boil over a medium heat. Reduce the heat to medium-low, then add the tamarind concentrate, pineapple, tomato, chillies and nam pla and cook for 10 minutes. Add the fish chunks and cook for 5 minutes, or until opaque and fork-tender.

4 Ladle the soup into small individual bowls. Scatter over the torn basil and saw leaves and drizzle with garlic oil to garnish. Serve immediately.

thai tom yum soup with fish

serves 6

- 1.5 litres/2¾ pints chicken stock
- 6 lemon grass stalks, crushed to release their flavour
- 3 tbsp very finely chopped coriander roots
- 10 kaffir lime leaves, central stalks torn off
- 1 red chilli, deseeded and finely chopped
- 2.5-cm/1-inch piece of galangal (or fresh ginger), peeled and thinly sliced
- 3 tbsp nam pla (fish sauce)
- 1 tbsp sugar
- 500 g/1 lb 2 oz raw prawns, shelled except for the tails
- 500 g/1 lb 2 oz firm white fish, such as cod or monkfish, chopped into bite-sized pieces
- 225 g/8 oz canned bamboo shoots or water chestnuts
- 12 cherry tomatoes, halved
- juice of 2 limes
- handful fresh coriander leaves and handful fresh basil leaves, chopped, to garnish

1 Pour the stock into a large saucepan and add the lemon grass, coriander roots, lime leaves, chilli, galangal, nam pla and sugar. Cover the saucepan. Bring to the boil, then reduce the heat and simmer for 10 minutes.

2 Add the prawns, fish and bamboo shoots and simmer for a further 4 minutes. Add the tomatoes and lime juice and check the seasoning, adding more nam pla and sugar, if necessary.

3 Remove and discard the lemon grass stalks, then divide the soup between six bowls and scatter over the coriander and basil leaves. Serve immediately.

thai salmon laksa

serves 4

- juice and zest of 2 limes
- 2 tbsp sunflower oil
- 1 red chilli, deseeded and finely chopped
- 4 garlic cloves, peeled and crushed
- 2.5-cm/1-inch piece fresh ginger, peeled and grated
- 1 tsp ground coriander
- small bunch of fresh coriander, plus extra to garnish
- 3 tbsp nam pla (fish sauce)
- 500 ml/18 fl oz vegetable or fish stock
- 850 ml/1½ pints canned coconut milk
- 3 carrots, peeled and very thinly sliced
- 400 g/14 oz noodles
- 1 tbsp sesame oil
- 1 tbsp vegetable oil
- 200 g/7 oz broccoli florets
- 500 g/1 lb 2 oz salmon fillet, skinned, boned and cut into slices half the width of a finger

1 Put the first 8 ingredients in a food processor or blender and blend to a paste.

2 Place a large saucepan over a medium heat and add the paste. Fry for 1 minute.

3 Add the stock, coconut milk and carrots and bring to the boil. Simmer while you cook the noodles according to the packet instructions.

4 Drain the noodles and return to the warm saucepan with a splash of sesame oil and vegetable oil. Cover.

5 Add the broccoli to the liquid, bring back to the boil and then turn off the heat and add the salmon slices, gently stirring them in. Leave to stand for 3 minutes.

6 Place a handful of noodles in each bowl, then ladle in the laksa. Sprinkle with coriander leaves and serve.

tuna chowder

serves 4

- 2 tbsp butter
- 1 large garlic clove, chopped
- 1 large onion, sliced
- 1 carrot, peeled and chopped
- 600 ml/1 pint fish stock
- 400 g/14 oz potatoes, peeled and cut into bite-sized chunks
- 400 g/14 oz canned chopped tomatoes
- 400 g/14 oz canned cannellini beans, drained
- 1 tbsp tomato purée
- 1 courgette, trimmed and chopped
- 225 g/8 oz canned tuna in brine, drained
- 1 tbsp chopped fresh basil
- 1 tbsp chopped fresh parsley
- 100 ml/3½ fl oz double cream
- salt and pepper
- sprigs of fresh basil, to garnish

1 Melt the butter in a large saucepan over a low heat. Add the garlic and onion and cook, stirring, for 3 minutes, until slightly softened. Add the carrot and cook for a further 5 minutes, stirring. Pour in the stock, then add the potatoes, tomatoes, beans and tomato purée. Season with salt and pepper. Bring to the boil, then reduce the heat, cover the pan and simmer for 20 minutes.

2 Add the courgette, tuna and chopped basil and parsley and cook for a further 15 minutes. Stir in the cream and cook very gently for a further 2 minutes.

3 Remove from the heat and ladle into individual serving bowls. Garnish with sprigs of fresh basil and serve immediately.

haddock & prawn chowder

serves 4
- 1 tbsp butter
- 1 onion, chopped
- 3 tbsp plain flour
- 500 ml/18 fl oz fish stock
- 1 bay leaf
- 500 ml/18 fl oz milk
- 2 tbsp dry white wine
- juice and grated rind of 1 lemon
- 450 g/1 lb haddock fillets, skinned
- 125 g/4½ oz frozen sweetcorn, defrosted
- 250 g/9 oz prawns, cooked and peeled
- 200 ml/7 fl oz double cream
- salt and pepper
- whole cooked prawns, to garnish
- fresh green salad, to serve

1 Melt the butter in a large saucepan over a medium heat. Add the onion and cook, stirring, for about 3 minutes, until slightly softened. In a bowl, mix the flour with enough stock to make a smooth paste and stir it into the pan. Cook, stirring, for 2 minutes, then gradually stir in the remaining stock. Add the bay leaf and season with salt and pepper. Bring to the boil, then lower the heat. Pour in the milk and wine, and stir in the lemon juice and grated rind. Simmer for 15 minutes.

2 Rinse the haddock under cold running water, then drain and cut into bite-sized chunks. Add them to the soup with the sweetcorn. Cook for 15 minutes, until the fish is tender and cooked through. Stir in the prawns and the cream. Cook for a further 2–3 minutes, then remove from the heat and discard the bay leaf.

3 Ladle into serving bowls, garnish with whole cooked prawns and serve with a fresh green salad.

bouillabaisse

serves 8

- 1 kg/2 lb 4 oz selection of at least 4 different firm white fish fillets, such as red mullet, snapper, sea bass, eel or monkfish, scaled and cleaned, but not skinned
- 100 ml/3½ fl oz olive oil
- 2 onions, finely chopped
- 1 fennel bulb, finely chopped
- 4 garlic cloves, crushed
- 1.2 kg/2 lb 10 oz canned chopped plum tomatoes
- 1.5 litres/2¾ pints fish stock
- pinch of saffron strands
- grated zest of 1 orange
- bouquet garni (see page 86)
- 500 g/1 lb 2 oz mussels, scrubbed and debearded
- 500 g/1 lb 2 oz cooked prawns, shell on
- salt and pepper
- crusty baguette and rouille, to serve

1 Carefully pin-bone the fish, then cut the fillets into bite-sized pieces.

2 Heat the oil in a very large frying pan or wide saucepan with a lid, add the onions and fennel and gently fry for about 15 minutes until soft. Add the garlic and fry for 2 minutes, then add the tomatoes and simmer for 2 minutes. Add the stock, saffron, orange zest and bouquet garni and bring to the boil. Simmer, uncovered, for 15 minutes.

3 Add the fish pieces, mussels and prawns and cover the pan. Simmer for a further 5–10 minutes until the mussels have opened. Discard any that remain closed. Check the seasoning.

4 Ladle into bowls and serve with pieces of crusty baguette and rouille.

smoked cod chowder

serves 4

- 25 g/1 oz butter
- 1 onion, finely chopped
- 1 small celery stick, finely diced
- 250 g/9 oz potatoes, diced
- 55 g/2 oz carrots, diced
- 300 ml/10 fl oz boiling water
- 350 g/12 oz smoked cod fillets, skinned and cut into bite-sized pieces
- 300 ml/10 fl oz milk
- salt and pepper
- fresh flat-leaf parsley sprigs, to garnish

1 Melt the butter in a large saucepan over a low heat, add the onion and celery and cook, stirring frequently, for 5 minutes, or until soft but not brown.

2 Add the potatoes, carrots, water and salt and pepper to taste. Bring to the boil, then reduce the heat and simmer for 10 minutes, or until the vegetables are tender. Add the fish to the chowder and cook for a further 10 minutes.

3 Pour in the milk and heat gently. Taste and adjust the seasoning, adding salt and pepper, if necessary. Ladle into warmed bowls and serve, garnished with parsley sprigs.

clam chowder

serves 4
- 900 g/2 lb live clams
- 4 bacon rashers, chopped
- 2 tbsp butter
- 1 onion, chopped
- 1 tbsp chopped fresh thyme
- 1 large potato, diced
- 300 ml/10 fl oz milk
- 1 bay leaf
- 375 ml/13 fl oz double cream
- 1 tbsp chopped fresh parsley
- salt and pepper

1 Scrub the clams and put them into a large saucepan with a splash of water. Cook over a high heat for 3–4 minutes until they open. Discard any that remain closed. Strain, reserving the cooking liquid. Leave until cool enough to handle, reserving 8 for a garnish.

2 Remove the clams from their shells, chopping them roughly if large, and reserve.

3 In a clean saucepan, fry the bacon until browned and crisp. Drain on kitchen paper. Add the butter to the same saucepan, and when it has melted, add the onion. Pan-fry for 4–5 minutes until soft but not coloured. Add the thyme and cook briefly before adding the diced potato, reserved clam cooking liquid, milk and bay leaf. Bring to the boil, then reduce the heat and leave to simmer for 10 minutes, or until the potato is just tender.

4 Discard the bay leaf, then transfer to a food processor or blender and blend until smooth, or push through a sieve into a bowl.

5 Add the clams, bacon and cream. Simmer for a further 2–3 minutes until heated through. Season to taste with salt and pepper. Stir in the chopped parsley and serve, garnished with the reserved clams in their shells.

quick scallop soup with pasta

serves 6

- 500 g/1 lb 2 oz shelled scallops
- 350 ml/12 fl oz milk
- 1.5 litres/2¾ pints vegetable stock
- 250 g/9 oz frozen petits pois
- 175 g/6 oz tagliolini
- 70 g/2½ oz butter
- 2 spring onions, finely chopped
- 175 ml/6 fl oz dry white wine
- 3 slices of prosciutto, cut into thin strips
- salt and pepper
- chopped fresh parsley, to garnish

1 Slice the scallops in half horizontally and season with salt and pepper.

2 Pour the milk and stock into a saucepan, add a pinch of salt and bring to the boil. Add the petit pois and pasta, bring back to the boil and cook for 8–10 minutes, until the taglialini is tender but still firm to the bite.

3 Meanwhile, melt the butter in a frying pan. Add the spring onions and cook over a low heat, stirring occasionally, for 3 minutes. Add the scallops and cook for 45 seconds on each side. Pour in the wine, add the prosciutto and cook for 2–3 minutes.

4 Stir the scallop mixture into the soup, taste and adjust the seasoning, if necessary, and garnish with the parsley. Serve immediately.

crab & vegetable soup

serves 4

- 2 tbsp chilli oil
- 1 garlic clove, chopped
- 4 spring onions, trimmed and sliced
- 2 red peppers, deseeded and chopped
- 1 tbsp grated fresh ginger
- 1 litre/1¾ pints fish stock
- 100 ml/3½ fl oz coconut milk
- 100 ml/3½ fl oz rice wine or sherry
- 2 tbsp lime juice
- 1 tbsp grated lime rind
- 6 kaffir lime leaves, finely shredded
- 300 g/10½ oz freshly cooked crabmeat
- 200 g/7 oz freshly cooked crab claws
- 150 g/5½ oz canned sweetcorn, drained
- 1 tbsp of chopped coriander, plus a few sprigs to garnish
- salt and pepper

1 Heat the oil in a large saucepan over a medium heat. Add the garlic and spring onions and cook, stirring, for about 3 minutes, until slightly softened. Add the red peppers and ginger and cook for a further 4 minutes, stirring. Pour in the stock and season with salt and pepper. Bring to the boil, then lower the heat. Pour in the coconut milk, rice wine and lime juice, and stir in the grated lime rind and kaffir lime leaves. Simmer for 15 minutes.

2 Add the crabmeat and crab claws to the soup with the sweetcorn and coriander. Cook the soup for 15 minutes, until the fish is tender and cooked right through.

3 Remove from the heat and ladle into serving bowls. Garnish with fresh coriander and serve.

asparagus & crab soup

serves 6

- 450 g/1 lb cooked fresh crabmeat
- 270 g/9½ oz fresh white or green asparagus, cut into 2-cm/¾-inch pieces
- 2 large egg whites, lightly beaten
- 1 tbsp cornflour
- 2 tbsp water
- salt and pepper
- 8 g/⅙ oz fresh coriander leaves, to garnish

chicken or crab stock

- 2.8 litres/5 pints water
- 900 g/2 lb meaty chicken bones or crab shells
- 25 g/1 oz fresh ginger, peeled and thinly sliced
- 4 spring onions, trimmed and crushed
- 2-3 tbsp nam pla (fish sauce)

1 For the stock, put the water and chicken bones or crab shells in a large saucepan and bring to the boil over a high heat. Reduce the heat to medium–low and add the ginger, spring onions and nam pla, then simmer for 1½ hours, or until reduced by about half, skimming off any scum. Strain the stock, discarding the solids, and remove any fat.

2 Pour the stock into a medium saucepan and bring to a gentle boil over a medium heat. Reduce the heat to medium–low, then add the crabmeat and asparagus, and season to taste with salt and pepper. Cover and simmer for 5 minutes, or until the flavours have blended.

3 Steadily pour the egg whites into the soup, stirring a few times, and simmer for a further 1–2 minutes, or until fully cooked. In a ladle, stir the cornflour and water together. Lower the ladle into the soup, then stir a few times. Cook until lightly thickened.

4 Ladle the soup into small individual bowls and scatter over the coriander to garnish, then serve immediately.

hot & sour prawn soup

serves 2

- 300 g/10½ oz raw prawns, peeled and deveined
- 2 tsp vegetable oil
- 2 fresh red chillies, sliced
- 1 garlic clove, sliced
- about 750 ml/1⅓ pints fish stock
- 4 thin slices fresh ginger
- 2 lemon grass stalks, bruised
- 5 kaffir lime leaves, shredded
- 2 tsp palm sugar or brown sugar
- 1 tbsp chilli oil
- handful of fresh coriander leaves
- dash of lime juice

1 Dry-fry the prawns in a frying pan or wok until they turn pink. Remove and set aside.

2 Heat the vegetable oil in the same pan, add the chillies and garlic and cook for 30 seconds.

3 Add the stock, ginger, lemon grass, lime leaves and sugar and simmer for 4 minutes. Add the reserved prawns with the chilli oil and coriander and cook for 1–2 minutes.

4 Stir in the lime juice and serve immediately.

prawn & vegetable bisque

serves 4
- 3 tbsp butter
- 1 garlic clove, chopped
- 1 onion, sliced
- 1 carrot, peeled and chopped
- 1 celery stick, trimmed and sliced
- 1.2 litres/2 pints fish stock
- 4 tbsp red wine
- 1 tbsp tomato purée
- 1 bay leaf
- 600 g/1 lb 5 oz prawns, peeled and deveined
- 100 ml/3½ fl oz double cream
- salt and pepper
- single cream and whole cooked prawns, to garnish

1 Melt the butter in a large saucepan over a medium heat. Add the garlic and onion and cook, stirring, for 3 minutes, until slightly softened. Add the carrot and celery and cook for a further 3 minutes, stirring. Pour in the stock and red wine, then add the tomato purée and bay leaf. Season with salt and pepper. Bring to the boil, then lower the heat and simmer for 20 minutes. Remove from the heat and leave to cool for 10 minutes, then remove and discard the bay leaf.

2 Transfer half of the soup into a food processor or blender and blend, in batches if necessary, until smooth. Return to the pan with the rest of the soup. Add the prawns and cook over a low heat for 5–6 minutes.

3 Stir in the cream and cook for a further 2 minutes, then remove from the heat and ladle into serving bowls. Garnish with swirls of single cream and whole cooked prawns and serve immediately.

three delicacy soup

serves 6

- 175 g/6 oz skinless, boneless chicken breast, very thinly sliced into strips
- 175 g/6 oz prawns, peeled and deveined, halved if large
- 1 tsp cornflour
- 2 tsp water
- 1 small egg white, lightly beaten
- pinch of salt
- 1 litre/1¾ pints vegetable stock
- 175 g/6 oz honey-roast ham, very thinly sliced into strips
- salt and pepper
- chopped spring onions or snipped fresh chives, to garnish

1 Mix together the chicken and prawns in a bowl. Mix the cornflour to a paste with the water in another bowl and add to the mixture, together with the egg white and the salt, stirring well to coat.

2 Bring the stock to the boil in a saucepan over a medium heat. Add the chicken and prawn mixture and the ham and bring back to the boil. Reduce the heat and simmer for 1 minute. Taste and adjust the seasoning, if necessary, and remove from the heat. Ladle into warmed bowls, garnish with spring onions and serve immediately.

Mmmm...

tomato & smoked shellfish soup

serves 4
- 700 ml/1¼ pints vegetable stock
- 6 ripe tomatoes, peeled, deseeded and chopped
- 1 cucumber, peeled, halved lengthways, deseeded and chopped
- 1 shallot, chopped
- 3 tbsp sherry vinegar
- 1 tsp sugar
- 1½ tsp Dijon mustard
- ¼ tsp Tabasco sauce or pinch of cayenne pepper
- 500 g/1 lb 2 oz smoked oysters or smoked mussels
- salt and pepper
- croûtons, to serve (see page 9)

1 Pour the stock into a bowl. Add the tomatoes, cucumber, shallot, vinegar, sugar, mustard, Tabasco sauce and smoked shellfish and stir well. Season to taste with salt and pepper, cover with clingfilm and chill for at least 2 hours.

2 To serve, stir the soup and taste and adjust the seasoning, if necessary. Ladle into bowls, sprinkle with the croûtons and serve.

mussel soup

serves 6
- 36 live mussels
- 150 ml/5 fl oz vegetable stock
- 300 ml/10 fl oz dry white wine
- ¼ onion, finely chopped
- ½ celery stick, finely chopped
- 5 tbsp chopped fresh flat-leaf parsley
- 600 ml/1 pint double cream
- pinch of cayenne pepper or dash of Tabasco sauce
- salt and pepper
- garlic and herb bread, toasted, to serve

1 Scrub the mussels under cold running water and pull off the 'beards'. Discard any with broken shells or that do not shut immediately when sharply tapped. Put them into a large saucepan, pour in the stock and wine and add the onion, celery and parsley. Cover and bring to the boil over a high heat. Cook, shaking the pan occasionally, for 3–5 minutes, until the shells have opened.

2 Remove the pan from the heat and lift out the mussels with a slotted spoon. Discard any that remain shut, shell the remainder and set aside for another dish.

3 Strain the soup into a clean pan and discard the contents of the strainer. Stir in the cream and cayenne pepper, season to taste with salt and pepper and leave to cool completely. Cover with clingfilm and chill for at least 3 hours.

4 To serve, stir the soup and taste and adjust the seasoning, if necessary. Ladle into bowls and serve immediately with garlic and herb bread.

Index